A Perfect Nightmare

A PERFECT NIGHTMARE

My Glittering Marriage
and How It Almost
Cost Me My Life

KAREN GOSBEE

sh.
SUTHERLAND
HOUSE
TORONTO, 2020

Sutherland House
416 Moore Ave., Suite 205
Toronto, ON M4G 1C9

First edition, October 2020

If you are interested in inviting one of our authors to a live event or
media appearance, please contact publicity@sutherlandhousebooks.com
and visit our website at sutherlandhousebooks.com for more
information about our authors and their schedules.

Manufactured in the United States
Cover designed by Lena Yang
Book composed by Karl Hunt
Library and Archives Canada Cataloguing in Publication
Title: A perfect nightmare : my glittering marriage and
how it almost cost me my life / Karen Gosbee.
Names: Gosbee, Karen, author.
Identifiers: Canadiana 20200296388 | ISBN 9781989555330 (softcover)
Subjects: LCSH: Gosbee, Karen. | LCSH: Gosbee, Karen—Marriage. |
LCSH: Abused wives—Canada—Biography. | LCSH: Wife abuse—Canada. |
LCSH: Marital violence—Canada. | LCGFT: Autobiographies.
Classification: LCC HV6626.23.C2 G67 2020 |
DDC 362.82/92092—dc23

ISBN 978-1-989555-33-0

TABLE OF CONTENTS

This book is dedicated to those who have been silenced.
May you find help, joy, and the strength to start
your own new chapter.

PROLOGUE

OVEMBER 12, 2017, and everything is coming to a head. I'm driving to the house as the sun is setting and the temperature dropping. In my mind, there is a sickening certitude. I know exactly where George will be and what he will have done. My brother Scott is in the car beside me. He called just as I was leaving and insisted he come along in case of a confrontation. My family has feared for my safety throughout my marriage, and their concerns have ramped up exponentially in the last week.

It's a Sunday. On Wednesday, I had asked George for a divorce after taking precautions for the safety of myself and my children. George had been violent over the course of our marriage and I did not expect him to respond well to my request. On Friday night, he had begun texting maniacally, a sure sign he was drinking again. We'd spent six hours hamster-wheeling, crossing the same ground over and over. He pleaded with me to meet him to look at papers about our finances. Every fibre in my body told me that would be a mistake. I was finally trusting my instincts. I woke the next morning to a stream of angry texts that had ended at 3 a.m.

As Scott and I approach the house, memories are flashing through my mind like a slideshow. George and I getting married in Turkey, so young and unprepared. The early fights. Me with my babies alone in big, beautiful houses. George drunk, asleep at the dinner table. George curled into a fetal position on the floor. George threatening suicide. George threatening me. I think of the decades I lived in terror of a certain look from him, how I was always walking on eggshells, waiting for the next outburst. I think of us fighting, us laughing, us fighting, then having sex. I think of the facade we constructed. Then I think about George's fist pounding my face in a Buenos Aires hotel room.

My most troubling memory was of the time I'd called the police after George pinned me down on the bathroom floor and tried to strangle me. My daughter Isla couldn't understand why I had called the police. Her father hadn't actually hurt me, she said. That was one of the many moments that led to my realization that it would be best for me to leave him, for my own safety and that of my children—what kind of an example was I setting?

I am keenly aware that, throughout our marriage, the wider world has seen the version of George Gosbee that he has wanted people to see: a successful man of forty-eight, known for his boundless energy, his towering business achievements, his enthusiasms, his grandiose gestures. He has built two investment companies from the ground. He was a co-owner of the Arizona Coyotes NHL hockey team, and has served two prime ministers. He climbs mountains. He hunts. He heli-skis. He reads and does yoga and cooks. We have a family, with three beautiful children: Instagram-perfect.

The other side he hides from view. Our family has lived under his "dark cloud" for decades. We live with the roller coaster of George's alcohol and substance misuse, his suicide attempts, his violence and abusive behaviour, and his repeated attempts to get better through therapy and rehab. He's been diagnosed with ADD, bi-polar disorder, and borderline personality disorder, and has been prescribed a long list of medications that he either doesn't take, or takes sporadically, fearing they'll dull what it is that makes him so successful. (It's not uncommon for mentally ill people to start and stop their meds or recovery plans.) The truth is that George's life has been one long fight: fighting for success, fighting for social approval, fighting his addictions, fighting me, fighting to stay alive, and fighting to keep these parts of himself from being discovered.

How things look is everything to George. He repeatedly tells me and the children that "perception is everything." He associates personal success with public accolades and external recognition, and does not feel any personal satisfaction without them. He believes his reputation will be destroyed if his mental illness, or his behaviours, are revealed. That terrifies him in a way that a cancer diagnosis or a heart condition would not. His obsession with optics is why I worried about his response to my asking for a divorce; but I could no longer live for the sake of appearances, and neither could my children.

I park the car and walk toward the house.

CHAPTER ONE

House on Fire

MY MARRIAGE WASN'T MY introduction to how addiction and mental illness can harm a family. My childhood was. My mother suffered from depression and what we now call substance use disorder. When I was twelve, she attempted suicide. Still, as a child growing up, I believed my family was normal. It was all I knew.

From the outside, my childhood probably looked idyllic and privileged. I grew up Karen Wilson, the youngest of three. My father, Fred, was a successful neurologist. My mother, Laura, was a beautiful stay-at home mom. In family photos of us on the beach, goofing in the backyard, in our kitchen with its '70s avocado-coloured appliances, we're always smiling. But my smile is forced and uncertain, a detail I now understand.

Life inside our two-story, green clapboard house on Marlboro Road in Edmonton was anything but idyllic. My mother's depression began after my birth. It was what we now know as postpartum depression; back then, it was "the baby blues." Like many women, my mother was prescribed Valium: "mother's little helper." And, like many women, she developed a dependency. She would regularly top the pills off with a glass or two of sherry—essentially doubling the depressants.

My mother's state wasn't helped by our family moving to a new neighbourhood when I was two so we could be closer to my dad's family. She was unsettled by that dislocation. And also by the fire. Our new home went up in flames after rags ignited in the furnace room. My crying in response to the smoke woke the household, according to family lore. We lived in an apartment while the house was repaired.

I was an anxious child, absorbing the tensions and sadness at home like a sponge. One of my first vivid memories is of my first grade teacher assigning parts for the Christmas play, and that I desperately wanted to be an angel. As she did so, a classmate burst into the room to report a pedestrian had been struck by a car outside. The person wasn't hurt, she said, but the woman driving the car was crying uncontrollably. My heart sank. I knew the driver had to be my mother, who'd just dropped me off. And I knew I wouldn't be an angel because I wasn't outgoing enough, and I'd have to manage my mother's sadness. When I got home, I found her sitting on the stairs sobbing. She'd often cry, perched there.

That year, my teachers worried because I wasn't talking or socializing. Testing found I had mild dyslexia, so it was decided I should repeat grade one at a private school. That created internal messaging: I was slow, I was stupid. I went to school only half a day and spent afternoons tending to my depressed mother. I blamed myself for her sadness because I required so much work. We'd have lunch, complete my homework, and then she'd go to bed, or collapse in exhaustion on the staircase, unable to make her way up. I'd watch horror movies that I still remember vividly—one featured a severed head, still breathing, in a paper bag in a freezer. Not good viewing for a child with anxiety.

Growing up with a parent afflicted by mental illness or addiction means life is always uncertain. You're on high alert, waiting, watching: Will my mom be sad? Will she be drunk and embarrass me? Often, that translates into hyper-vigilance in adulthood. Today, I know what's going on in any room I'm in: who's angry with whom, who's flirting with whom, how many drinks someone's had.

My siblings and I avoided home as much as we could. I didn't have many friends because bringing them home to play wasn't an option. I'd look longingly at my classmates whose families seemed happy and harmonious. My dad coped by not coming home until we'd all gone to bed. When he was home, my parents bickered constantly, oblivious to our presence and discomfort. In time, we became immune to their behaviour. We normalized it, thinking all parents had a mutual disgust and lack of respect for one another. Normal is whatever you're used to.

Our family never discussed what was going on. It just never came up. My brother and sister and I communicated non-verbally: whoever was first through the door would go to talk to our mom. If she was wasted, you'd avoid her. The next person through the door would go to the first sibling. If they gave you the silent signal of a glass raised to the mouth, you'd stay away.

Unable to control what was happening around me, I turned my anger and self-hatred inward, as children do in such environments. I decided I was fat. I recall my seven-year-old self sitting on the side of a bathtub in a motel in Moose Jaw, Saskatchewan, where the family was attending a family reunion. I hated family functions. I was always afraid that my mom would get drunk, as she was this time. I remember looking at the flesh of my thighs in self-disgust and crying uncontrollably. My father, furious because I wasn't socializing, dragged me back to the party. My delusion of being overweight would manifest as full-blown bulimia when I was a teen.

Generally, though, we didn't travel much. We went to Disneyland, and took a trip to Hawaii when I was ten that I remember as "National Lampoon Goes to Maui." My mother was drunk the entire time. My dad had brought a good friend with severe cerebral palsy on the trip, who was an intelligent, kind man who required a lot of physical space and patience to be around, as did my mother. Shortly after we all arrived, an epic storm moved in—the worst in a century—leaving us stuck indoors. My dad escaped by helping the community sandbag. My escape was reading: *Princess Daisy* by Judith Krantz, and Judy Blume's *Are You There God? It's Me, Margaret.* Anything I could get my ten-year-old hands on.

Our mother's illness meant we looked, disproportionately, for attention and approval from my dad. He was an outdoor enthusiast and a Cub Scout leader, activities he shared with my brother, Scott, who also became a neurologist. My sister, Kathy, was the "good daughter," an honours student who became an occupational therapist. I was jealous of her and always compared myself to her, to my detriment. I felt alone and believed I didn't get the same support she did. If anything went wrong in the house, it was assumed it was my fault. I was so desperate for attention from my dad, good or bad, that I was happy to play the black sheep.

* * *

I was twelve in the summer of 1982, and my parents were fighting all the time. My mother was numbed out 24/7 and my father was consistently annoyed. We had been forced to spend more time with each other during the "summer break," which only resulted in more conflict.

One evening started like most others: my father and mother had a big fight about her drinking. They retreated to the bedroom and we could hear screams, cries, and physical commotion, and then silence. That night, my father slept in another room. In the morning, with the sun barely rising, he went for a walk. When he returned, he went into my mother's room to discover she had overdosed on pills, stabbed herself with scissors, and fallen into a deep, drugged sleep. I remember my dread and indifference when my dad told us not to be afraid, that he'd called the paramedics. I just wanted their fighting to over. I'd lost all faith that it would. Once the commotion had passed, I prepared myself breakfast like every other morning.

It wasn't my mother's first brush with suicide. When I was eight, she'd said, "I'm going away to a place I don't need a suitcase." I knew what she meant, and begged her not to do anything. I told her I loved her and would miss her. But I also harboured an anger I was unable to express: I hated what she was doing to herself and to the family. I'd frantically search for the pills hidden in her purse and throughout the house. I'd dump them down the toilet, then cross my fingers that, without her supply, she'd stop.

When I was ten, my mother threatened to jump off the roof; my dad had to pull her in a few times. Our biggest worry was "What will the neighbours think?" By that time, my dad was regularly falling asleep in the family room watching *M.A.S.H* or *Taxi*. I'd drag my mattress into my sister's room and we'd sleep together, a pattern I'd see later see with myself and my own children.

After her overdose, my mother was put into a medically induced coma and nearly died. My dad didn't sugarcoat it when he told us she probably wouldn't survive. I didn't know how to react. I was glad she was out of the house. I had so much bottled-up anger.

Then, out of the blue, I received an unexpected gift thanks to an argument that arose between my father's sisters. My Auntie Sheila, a psychologist, said that even if my mother came out of the coma, she'd probably never overcome her addiction. My Auntie Beth, a nurse, responded angrily: "You can't say that to the girls; you're taking away all of their hope."

Listening to them made me realize that there were two sides, not just the one I'd been locked into. Until then, I had seen myself as the powerless victim in a hopeless situation. Now, there was a chance that I could make sense of what happened. I had something to work towards, regardless of how it turned out.

I wanted to see my mother, although my siblings weren't interested. Part of it was curiosity: I'd never seen anyone in a coma. My dad and I went to the intensive care ward at the University of Alberta Hospital. Looking down at my mother, I grabbed her hand. Later, she told me she felt my touch and that it was the persuasion she needed to come back and be a parent to her children. She wanted another chance.

That was the beginning of me rebuilding a close relationship with my mother, one I treasure today. I visited her in the psychiatric ward after she was moved out of intensive care, and we talked for hours. I discovered we share a dark sense of humour, a sensibility that my father didn't appreciate. For me, it was a survival skill I still use today.

I learned about her early life. My mother grew up the youngest of ten in a house without plumbing. And she had ambition: she grew up to be a lab technician who wanted to travel the world. She met my father through a work colleague, when my dad was in medical school. He told my mom, "Okay, you travel and come back to be the wife of a physician." She did. My mom saw being a doctor's wife as life in the big leagues.

She hadn't anticipated everything turning out as it did. Who grows up expecting to have major depression and substance misuse problems? She later told me of her near-death experience, that she'd seen a light and realized she could choose to go toward it or come back. She also experienced a flashback of being sexually abused by her father as a child, something she would come to understand had fueled her depression. Valium fueled it, too, but unresolved sexual abuse was the bigger issue.

While she was in treatment, my father took a "tough love" approach with my mother. He handed her a restraining order, and told her she couldn't come back or see the children until she proved she was committed to change. To her credit, she did the difficult work, which included a stint in one of the province's first rehabilitation programs: the Henwood Treatment Centre outside of Edmonton.

My mother's story is proof family dynamics can change. She was in rehab for a month. She next went to live in a halfway house, another of my father's stipulations: he wanted her to see what her life could look like if she wasn't with the family. She had four roommates, all Indigenous women who'd been prostitutes; some had been heroin addicts. They were all very warm and supportive of my mother and me and far more empathetic, I felt, that most of the people I came across in my world. It was my introduction to the intersections of poverty, race, and addiction, and I never looked at people's problems and vulnerabilities the same way after that.

While my mother was at Henwood, it was suggested that the rest of the family could benefit from therapy, too. We lasted one session. The therapist tried to make my dad see how he was responsible for some of what was going on. My dad didn't like being put on the spot, and that was that. We were all relieved not to have to go, a typical reaction among family members who aren't the ones addicted: "For God's sake, we've been subject to your behaviour for so long, why do we have to do work now? It's not our problem." Of course, it was our problem. We had a lot of familial dysfunction that needed to be addressed.

When my mother came home, she did everything she could to improve herself and grow. She became certified to teach Smoke Enders, a smoking-cessation program. Legislation banning smoking in the workplace was being passed and corporations wanted to help employees quit. In time, she was responsible for all of Alberta. She joined Toastmasters and also began exercising, which for her was probably the biggest change of all.

A family ritual started at that time of walking around the block after dinner. On one of these walks with my mother and father one summer evening in 1986, I mentioned that a neighbour was having an affair. My father became flustered, which tripped my hyper-intuitive senses. I asked a couple of questions the next day at his office and quickly figured out that, while my mother was grappling with illness, my dad had been involved in a long-term affair. He'd checked out of the marriage, while my mom was trying desperately to make it work. I was the only one to confront him.

By this time, my dad and I were constantly clashing. I decided everything was his fault. "Mom's getting her shit together," I'd tell him. "What are you doing?" Today, I don't see the situation as black-and-white. I don't blame my dad. He was doing the best he could.

School remained a problem for me. I began skipping class in grade six, the year my mother attempted suicide, successfully forging my mother's signature on notes of absence. Then I'd skip exams because I was anxious about failing because I'd missed class. My behaviour was a red flag that someone needed to follow-up on because it was being caused by an actual illness on my part; it just wasn't the flu or measles. Trauma affects children and disrupts the architecture of a developing brain, and I've learned a lot since then about how it works. At the time, however, my actions just seemed like a character failing on my part.[1]

I kept my head above water by playing sports: badminton, basketball, baseball, track and field, and, later, volleyball for Team Alberta. After my mother's suicide attempt, I began to run around the block to think, and to de-stress. I still run almost every day. It's calming: time that is mine alone.

As a teen, I was timid and constantly frightened. I never looked people in the eye when I spoke to them. People would instruct me to smile, rather than ask why I didn't. When my high-school volleyball coach pulled me

---

1 The Centers for Disease Control's Adverse Childhood Experiences (ACE) Study, led by Dr. Vincent Felitti in the mid-1990s, helped us understand that childhood trauma increases health risks as well as social and emotional problems in adulthood—obesity, depression, suicide, violent behaviour, and even being a victim of violence. We also know childhood trauma is common amongst middle-class, college-educated people, although affluent populations tend to be overlooked because of class bias. Money doesn't make someone a more competent parent, though it does offer resources to create a facade, and hire help.

aside to say I may not make first line for grade twelve, my father told me it was good news, and told me I should quit sports. He felt they distracted from doing well in school. I listened to him and quit volleyball, but I lost that support group and had too much free time, and so my grades suffered more, not less. Boys were in the picture, but never a huge focus for me.

My dad tried the same "tough love" approach on me that had worked on my mother. He'd tell me I'd never amount to anything more than a hairdresser: the same tactic his own father had used on my Aunt Sheila, who then went on to become a psychologist. He was trying to get me to set goals, but his comments only stoked my insecurity. One upshot is that I'm very good at doing my own hair, and that of friends and kids. I probably would have been an excellent hair stylist.

By the time I was sixteen, tensions with my father had reached a point where it was decided I should stay with his mother, my Gran, who lived a block over. She had multiple sclerosis, a degenerative nerve disease, her housekeeper had recently quit, and she needed help until they hired another one.

My grandmother was an amazing person. She was the fourth woman in Alberta to receive a university degree, which she followed up with a nursing degree at the University of British Columbia. She had a zest for life. She liked to read, play bridge, and entertain. She called me "glamour puss" and became a mentor to me, encouraging my artistic aspirations. Since the sixth grade, I'd enjoyed drawing and studying art and art history, and I'd received praise and encouragement from teachers for my skill. I went through the typical teenage Impressionists phase, loving Van Gogh in part because we shared a birthday. I basked in my grandmother's positive attention, and ended up living with her until I moved to Calgary to attend university.

Over time, my relationship with my dad improved. He began focusing on my mother more, and home life became more harmonious. One area of continued friction with my father, however, was the subject of what I should study in university. In our home, you were a lawyer, a doctor, or an engineer. Seeking my father's approval, I believed I wanted to become a doctor, although my grades at the time definitely wouldn't get me into medical school. Studying fine art is what I wanted for myself, but he saw no money or future in it. He told me he'd pay my tuition if I took science or attended the University of Alberta and lived at home. That wasn't an option. My grades were too low. Besides, I needed to get away, from him and from everything.

I took a year off, saved money, and was accepted into the arts program at the University of Calgary. It should have been a happy moment, but I harboured a lot of shame and self-hatred for not meeting my father's and, by extension, my own academic standards.

Looking back now, I can see how the imprint of my childhood travelled with me to Calgary and created the training wheels for my marriage. I was a girl who sought affirmation, who didn't feel worthy or smart enough. I didn't know how to ask for love and support, or how to give it, least of all to myself. And I thought that it was normal for families to keep secrets.

CHAPTER TWO

Introducing George

WHEN PEOPLE TALK ABOUT GEORGE, they always mention his laugh. He had a memorable, rat-tat-tat-tat laugh, like a friendly machine gun. Our eldest son John called it a "rolling, infectious chuckle." Others have described it as "cackling" and even "hyena-like."

Laughter bonded George and me when we met in 1991 at the University of Calgary. I had heard about him before we met. He was the guy who threw parties in bars, an early example of his entrepreneurial instincts. He'd strike a deal with some establishment to give him exclusive access from around three in afternoon until eight at night. In return, he promised to fill the place with students. Tickets cost twenty dollars for access to a party and a drink, and the bar took a percentage of the profits. The margins were crazy good. I had friends in the service industry who told me to show up at eight so I wouldn't have to spend twenty dollars, and I did. I was clearly my father's daughter: frugal.

No one partied harder at George's parties than George. Before I'd actually met him, I was walking through the parking lot of a popular Calgary bar and tripped over something. "What is that?" I said, thinking it was a parking curb. It was George. He was drunk. It wasn't uncommon for bar staff to stow his body, passed out, behind the bar, then load him into a taxi and send him home. Drinking a lot was normal in my crowd, but George took it to extremes.

He was also known as the guy with the brain tumor. He'd taken time off from studying commerce when he was twenty-one to have surgery on a benign cyst the size of a golf ball. When I returned home for Christmas in second year, my dad asked if I knew a George Gosbee. He and a neurologist colleague had been talking about this kid in Calgary who'd had an operation involving a shunt inserted in his brain. "Yeah," I said. "He ran for VP of the student's union but he's more famous for the parties he throws."

I'd started out studying at the University of Calgary. But due to a fluky series of events, before George and I were introduced, I'd transferred to another Calgary university, Mount Royal, to study interior design. At the time, I'd been living with the daughter of my dad's best friend (the guy who had set up my parents).[2] My roommate had applied to the interior-design program at Mount Royal, but couldn't draw. I could draw, so I drew her portfolio. Then she decided to become a cop. I mailed in the application out of curiosity to see if I'd be accepted, using my parent's Edmonton address. One day, my father, with that disregard for boundaries common in troubled families, called to tell me he'd opened my mail and that I'd been accepted.

My dad was supportive. He thought studying interior design, unlike an arts degree, was a route to a job. He offered to pay for the program. Given that I was subsisting on packaged ramen, wondering how to make ends meet, I jumped at the offer. I figured I'd get a diploma and work as an interior designer while I finished university. My dad's belief that self-worth came with a university degree was ingrained into me.

Shortly after my dad asked me about George that Christmas, I bumped into him at a Calgary bar called Claudio's. He hadn't gone to school that semester, and was in post-surgery rehab. I'd completed my course and was working for a decor store, Chintz & Co., to see if design was what I really wanted to do. I asked him about his health, and we started chatting.

---

2 My roommate's mother had been my mother's former lab colleague, who had had mental health issues and addiction problems of her own. She had died of what appeared to be suicide, although the official version was "accidental overdose." Again, no one talked about it.

I was immediately attracted to George's personality. He was entertaining, very smart, and extremely confident. He seemed to know everything. Even if a lot of it was just salesmanship on his part, he was convincing, whether he was talking about the economy or politics or some random theory he had. And he was passionate with a strong sense of personal destiny, a conviction that he was going to make it that I also found attractive. We talked easily to one another, and laughed a lot.

It was not a love-at-first-sight, head-over-heels attraction. George was one of those men who grew into his looks as he aged. Back then, he had long, wavy, side-parted hair and he wore these big, red-framed, Sally Jessy Raphael-like glasses. I believe he was wearing a red sports coat with shoulder pads that night that I called his "Solid Gold" jacket (after the TV dance show) and later banned him from wearing. He was tall, 6'1", but incredibly skinny after the surgery. His pencil neck and Adam's apple were his most distinguishing characteristics.

Nevertheless, the connection was genuine. I would learn in time that I was his type: a tall, skinny blonde, not terribly confident or assertive, willing to take his lead. I asked him to a Christmas party at my dad's best friend's house, which I later learned was next door to George's parents' house. He said he couldn't. I sensed he was hiding something, so I asked him about it. He admitted he was engaged to be married.

The engagement had happened just before his surgery, he said, when it seemed like a life-or-death situation and emotions were running high. She was nineteen, he was twenty-one. Now he felt trapped. I didn't judge him; I didn't think "what a creep" for asking me out earlier. I told him I was sorry to hear it, and I was.

A few months later, George turned up at Chintz & Co. where he and his fiancée had been registered. He was newly single; his fiancée had broken off the engagement days before the wedding. He went to the clerk they'd been working with and asked if she could set him up with me. I was unsure. I'd been hearing rumors about George: how he'd somehow cashed in on life insurance, how he'd been going to school and simultaneously working at the brokerage Peters & Co., how he'd never finished his degree. Nothing concrete, nothing devastating. It's that there were just so many conflicting stories that he seemed a bit sketchy. My co-worker convinced me to give him a chance. He got us tickets to see Sarah McLachlan, who I really like, and we had fun.

Afterward, we attended the opening of Teatro, a popular Calgary restaurant. As we walked through the crowd, a drunk woman (who later became a friend) spilled red wine over my white outfit. She blamed me for the accident, and started to mock what I was wearing with her friends. George, naturally, was upset about this. "You're so calm," he said. He wanted to know where I learned these skills. I told him I'd taken a behavioural modification course with my mother that provided useful tools for daily living. He told me he wanted those same skills. He wanted to be like me, and to be around me all the time.

George and I began dating regularly in November of 1993. After I returned from spending Christmas with my family, he announced he wanted us to become serious. I wasn't sure if I wanted that. I still didn't know if I completely trusted him. There had been hints that George's idea of an exclusive relationship was more about exclusivity on my part than on his. He also had a temper. He'd been thrown off Alberta's badminton team for displays of anger, and I'd once felt compelled to send him a letter after he'd behaved badly, becoming enraged over something totally insignificant in a way that troubled me.

The flip side was that I had a high tolerance for unhealthy behaviours. I'd grown up amid secrets. I'd grown up amid drama and trauma. Psychologically healthy people bored me—they weren't what I knew. In this weird way, George's failings were attractive to me. I was comfortable around him and most of the time he was fun. I definitely had feelings for him.

With all this in mind, I came up with a compromise. I suggested we travel in May to Turkey, someplace I'd wanted to go since studying about it in my art history classes. "Let's see if we're compatible," I told him. He agreed.

Then, in March, everything changed. I found out I was pregnant. We had generally used condoms but, clearly, we hadn't been careful enough.

When I found out, I went for a long walk and lay down on the grass and stared at the sky. I watched the clouds pass me by. I thought of all the times I had gone running past the very place where I lay. I was always running, I realized, but there was no way I could run away from this. He or she would need me.

I knew I would have the baby. Having an abortion wasn't an option for me, personally. I'd driven a friend to an appointment to terminate her pregnancy a few months earlier; when I picked her up, I was the emotional one, thinking I couldn't have done it.

When I told George about the pregnancy, I told him I'd deal with the baby and take full responsibility. "I don't expect you to be by my side," I said. His reaction surprised me. "This is the best news," he said. "I make enough money. I can support the baby. We'll make this work." We didn't discuss marriage, which wasn't on my horizon.

The next step was to break the news to our parents. I had already met George's parents, John and Edna. They had been born in Prince Edward Island. Edna was the sixth of seven children. John had had polio when he was young, and the physical aftereffects meant he couldn't take over the Gosbee lobster fishing enterprise, so the family business ended there. He was told he'd have to rely on his brains over his brawn, and eventually earned a PhD in physiology. When he realized most of the available jobs in that line were with big American pharma companies, he applied to medical school to stay in Canada. George was born in Kingston, Ontario, where his parents had moved to cover her pregnancy. The family later moved to Calgary, where John completed his medical degree.

George's childhood was the polar opposite of mine. His parents were hands-on and supportive. They encouraged him to be entrepreneurial, and helped him to buy his first mining stock at a young age, to get patents on his inventions, to start a T-shirt company. I heard all of the stories of him being a hyperactive kid and a born leader. His nickname was "the Tasmanian Devil," after the Looney Tunes character.

My parents, however, hadn't met George yet, and he insisted we not break the pregnancy news to them over the phone. George cared deeply about how everything looked. He wanted to create the perfect setting, so he arranged to meet my parents at the Emerald Lake Lodge, a beautiful hotel in the Rockies, two-and-a-half hours from Calgary. After we told them the baby news, my parents wanted to know if George's parents knew. George's dad did, we said, but his mother didn't.

My dad took out the little notebook he carried everywhere. "Okay, great," he said, turning to George. "What's your last name?" He wrote it down. George loved to tell that story.

The plan was to stay overnight, then meet up again in Banff for lunch on the way home. We got to the restaurant, and waited, and waited. This was before cellphones, and we had no idea of where my parents were. They never showed. We drove back to George's parents' house in Calgary and found my parents sitting in the living room. They had wanted to get there ahead of us and talk adult-to-adult.

"We've talked. You're having our grandchild," they announced. "Go on your trip. You'll get married when you get back."

The scene was beyond tense. George's mother was angry and hurt that she'd been left in the dark about the pregnancy. George was furious at my mom and dad, and not without reason. The situation was another result of my family's boundary problems, and my father's own control issues, as he was concerned was that we wouldn't make the "right" decision. But it wasn't all Fred and Laura's fault, as George insisted. I tried to convince him they were just looking out for our best interests, but that made him more angry. He went into a quiet sulk.

In May, we traveled to Turkey for ten days, landing in Ankara. The trip started well. George's friend, Birol Fisecki, met us at the airport. He was someone I knew from volleyball and summer camp, and it was terrific to see him. Birol's father was Turkish, his mother English, and they had houses in Kemer, on the southern coast of Turkey, and in Calgary because they wanted their kids raised in Canada. We stayed in Kemer with Birol's parents, who were warm, wonderful hosts.

Soon after we arrived in Kemer, Birol took us out to celebrate at a boat party. I wasn't drinking, so I spent the night watching George drink enough for us both. We returned home past midnight, exhausted. George woke up the next morning badly hungover and disoriented. "Turn off the water, turn off the water," he moaned. When I looked out the window, I saw that their beautiful house on the Mediterranean coast was on top of a former grain mill with one of those churning paddle wheels once used to grind the flour. That was the source of the noise.

There were a few tense moments while travelling. George was hungover at breakfast one morning while we were in Cappadocia, a beautiful region with honeycomb rock formations and famous "fairy chimneys." He became angry when I took too long to finish eating; I tried to comply. *I have to figure out how not to be like this if I'm going to be with this man*, I thought to myself, which became my pattern. My response to George was never to say: "Easy, calm down." It was always internal, to myself: *I have to adjust.*

Three days before we were to go home and navigate wedding planning with our parents, George asked Birol if we could marry in Turkey. Thanks to Birol's family connections, we organized a wedding in forty-eight hours, got the wedding certificate, and bought rings and a cake. I purchased a white sundress and shoes. George bought a linen vest and pants. We married on Friday, May 13, at Kemer's city hall. We joked about the timing, but I optimistically deflected any negativity. "Thirteen is my lucky number," I announced.

I can't say I was filled with excitement to be married to George. It felt more like a *fait accompli*. There were parts I was quite happy about—I liked the idea of us building a life together, building a family, and I thought it would be good for me if I could absorb some of his confidence. But even as we organized the wedding, I was thinking, "If it doesn't work out, we can always get divorced."

Later, George told everyone we married at nearby Phaselis, a scenic ancient Roman port where we took our wedding pictures. He wanted our wedding to sound more fabulous than it was. I went along with his version to make him happy. George always included the detail about Turkey and Greece arguing whether Phaselis was the original Mount Olympus when he told the story.

Birol's parents threw a reception at their house. The entire village, maybe thirty people, showed up. Everyone got wasted, except me, being pregnant, and they all seemed to have a wonderful time. Then it was time to go home. On our way back to Calgary, we stopped for a night in Berlin. At the hotel, George asked a waiter if there were any good places to go. I laughed at his question, thinking to myself, "Of course there are good places to go. This is Berlin." My amusement was met by George's hard, cold stare.

We returned to our room and George exploded with a fury I'd never seen from him. "You made me look like an idiot," he shouted. He continued yelling. Finally, I locked myself in the bathroom, propping myself up on the long counter. I soaked my feet in the sink while George berated me from the other side of the door. My mind was caught in a loop of self-blame. *I shouldn't have laughed at him*, I thought. *I'd been insensitive. It was wrong of me to make him feel inadequate.* Finally, I heard the hotel door shut.

I stayed sitting in the bathroom, maybe for forty-five minutes or maybe two hours. I remember staring at myself in the mirror, newly married, three months' pregnant at age twenty-four, unsure of who I was, what was happening, or what I should do about it. I finally went to bed and fell into such a deep sleep that I didn't hear George return. When we woke the next morning, we had a plane to catch, and parents to deal with on our return. We never spoke of the evening again.

CHAPTER THREE

White Picket Fence

MY ANXIETY WAS OFF THE CHARTS as our plane approached Calgary. Our families were waiting, expecting to plan our wedding. We were also smuggling in artifacts we'd bought (two hockey bags full of old rugs, vases, kitchen implements, and so on). It was against Turkish law to take anything out of the country that was forty years or older; that's difficult in a land where everything seems at least a century old, and we were definitely over the line. George confidently took control, which was fine with me. I'm a terrible liar. My face and sweaty palms give me away.

"Follow me," he instructed, as he piled hockey bags on a cart and shifted into his charming salesman mode. When the customs officer asked what we had to declare, George announced we were newlyweds. Everyone showered us with congratulations instead of combing through our contraband. George was masterful at shielding his behaviours through sleight of hand.

My nerves calmed. My sister Kathy, whom I was living with at the time, was at the airport to meet me, and George's mom and dad were there for him. We broke the news of our wedding to a chorus of hesitant "Congratulations." Then, a defining moment: Which car do I go in? Kathy's? Or George's parents' car? I was no longer Karen Wilson, I realized. I was a Gosbee. Looking back, I was more torn about not going with my sister and her reluctant reaction than I was about George's outburst the night before.

We moved into the house George owned in Calgary's Kensington neighbourhood, where he'd lived with his former fiancée. The house was built in 1912 and was literally surrounded by a white-picket fence, straight out of *Leave it to Beaver*. Maybe that's why I always felt like a bit of an imposter there, as though I was playing house.

I was still working at Chintz & Co., with plans to go back to school after the baby was born in November. A professor encouraged me to enroll in environmental design, a new program at the time. I'd be accepted as a mature student because of my interior-design diploma, he said. I wasn't used to that kind of support and was buoyed by it.

George's reaction was simple: "No way!" He wanted me to have the baby and become a full-time mom. "We're on the same page," he assured me. "You'll stay at home. I'll make the money." Most women would die to have this opportunity, he told me. I didn't fight it.

"I'm so lucky," I told myself.

George remained angry about our parents' pregnancy ambush and would vilify my dad, with whom I still had a choppy relationship. He'd mock my father's frugality and gleefully report back any negative comments he made about me. Our first Christmas together, George gave me a Rolex watch. My dad, who wouldn't buy a Rolex in a million years, was confounded, George told me. He said that my dad asked him why he spent so much money on me. George took that as a demonstration that my family didn't appreciate me. I, too, took it as a comment on my worth.

Those first months of marriage also saw the beginning of what I'd call my night terrors. The fact that I slept soundly annoyed George. I'd be in a deep sleep and would wake to George angrily thrashing about. At first, I wouldn't know where I was. My heart would be beating out of my chest, like you see in cartoons. George blamed my pregnancy and my snoring, not the alcohol he'd consumed earlier in the evening, for disrupting his sleep. The solution, as he saw it, was for me to change my sleeping patterns. I learned to cope by lying completely still on my back, not moving a muscle, while trying to quiet my fears. Fear always exhausted me, so I'd usually fall back asleep within forty-five minutes, after I was confident George had fallen asleep as well.

John's birth in November of 1994 changed everything for me. Before motherhood, I'd been depressed much of the time, emotionally flat except when suffering from overwhelming anxiety. After his birth, those heavy feelings lifted. I experienced the opposite of post-partum depression: it was like a helium lift. Becoming a caregiver at age twenty-four gave me definition I'd never known before. I had a role, a purpose. Every moment of every day, I knew what I was supposed to be doing. I was completely focused on being John's mother. I enjoyed doing it, and I had no time for moping or self-pity. It helped that John was a wonderful baby, super-cute and easy to care for.

The relationship that became more complicated after childbirth was my relationship with George. He liked the idea of being a father, although in a very traditional role. He didn't like changing diapers, and never did. He also didn't feel comfortable minding John by himself. That I learned when I asked him to look after the baby so I could attend a friend's shower. While I was out, George kept calling me, unsure of what to do. When I got home, he was furious. "Do not leave me alone with the baby again," he said.

I never did, which a friend called me out on later: "You're not giving him the opportunity to be a dad," she said. I saw her point but I didn't have a choice. It was not a fight I was going to win.

George also felt competition for my affection. "You spend more time with John than me," he'd say. He was right, and I imagine it was difficult for him, but John was an infant, and George was supposed to be a grown-up. I knew where my focus should be.

In the spring of 1995, I went back to school, one night class a week. It was a compromise. I'd wanted to go full time, but George wanted me at home. His mother cared for the baby when I went to school, and George watched TV. She adored John and was happy to do it. My mother-in-law also adhered to traditional roles as a wife. Once, she told me it was my job to look after our child and George, and that I should wake at 5:30 a.m. to make George breakfast before work.

I enrolled in two courses, then dropped out due to rising tensions at home. George made it clear he was unhappy I'd gone back to school, and we fought about it in a way that became increasingly explosive. Couples, even newlyweds, know the locations of one other's tender spots, where to prod to get a response. There's a line from the Jeffrey Eugenides' short story "Baster," about how couples can get their "dark hooks" into one another: "Some dark hook in our brains, which no one could see, linked us up."

It was like that with us. My dark hooks were insecurity about my intelligence and my lack of education, and George's attacks focused on me being "uneducated." He'd say: "You're so fucking stupid, you don't know anything," or mock me by cruelly imitating the voice of someone with special needs: "Look at me, I'm Karen Wilson, the stupidest member of the Wilson family. I'm a fucking idiot."

Anything that went wrong would be my fault: "If you could do only this or that, we wouldn't have a problem," or "You have to commit to us and make us better." He'd say I wasn't attentive enough to him. He'd also say he treated me better than my family did. If I defended my family, he'd become angry. All of his attacks were designed to belittle me and assert his dominance in the relationship.

Here's where it gets complicated, and where I would blame myself: I knew what George's buttons were as well. For all of his bravado, he harboured deep insecurities. Poor body image was one. Before we met, he took steroids—human growth hormone, or HGH—to build muscle. His supplier was one of the dealers that infested Calgary after the 1988 Olympics, a former Jamaican athlete turned steroid dealer. George began using again in the mid-1990s, this time a more highly concentrated HGH that was smuggled in from the United States. His obsession with bulking up would be the source of an explosive reaction to one of the first meals I made after we married: a low-fat beef and broccoli stir-fry with salty black bean sauce. I was proud of it. After one taste, he flipped out. "Don't cook me this shit again," he yelled. "It is one of the worst meals I've ever had." He didn't like that it was "low-fat."

When I really wanted to get under his skin, I would say that certain people didn't like him, and play on his fear of being left out. There were, in fact, nice, decent, neighbourly people we knew who didn't want anything to do with George, and that hurt him. It didn't help for me to point this out.

We fought quite a bit: not every day, but every week or two. The fights were all-or-nothing. We'd push it to the limit; we'd talk about divorcing.

When we made up, we'd talk about having another kid. We'd go to bed and I would think that matters had been resolved, but then wake up to fight another day. George wasn't happy until I had cried or he had cried. Then, he'd feel awful and apologize and try to make up for it.

If you'd asked me if I was afraid of him, I would have said I was simply exhausted by it all. It was a passionate relationship, with all kinds of power and control dynamics. Not surprisingly, we also had good sex. Part of me fed off the drama of it all because, again, it was what I knew. The more rational part of me knew the fighting was a problem but figured it would abate as we learned to live together. I thought I could change his behaviour, help him modify his drinking. After all, my mother had changed so there was no reason George couldn't. He was young and dynamic, and he was having a lot of success elsewhere in his life.

To the outside world, George was indeed thriving. Calgary is an oil and gas town, which means it's a city of boom and bust. When I met George, it was boom. He continued working at Peters & Co. after university. A gifted salesman, he quickly became a top commission earner. He asked his bosses for the territory of New York City to develop, and they agreed. There was a growing market on Wall St. for Calgary-based junior oil-and-gas stocks, and George was the perfect person to sell them. He traveled down one week of every month, leaving on a Saturday and returning on a Wednesday.

In 1995, he was invited to be a Peters & Co. director, which required coming up with $200,000 to invest in the firm. In the brokerage world, $200,000 isn't a lot of money. It was for us. Our bank was willing to float a loan, but only if George had someone co-sign. He went to his dad, who turned him down because he'd had a bad experience loaning money to family. Mortified, George went to my dad—the "awful dad," in his books—who agreed. George wasn't comfortable with that arrangement in the end, so he found another bank that would loan him the money without a co-signer.

When George had bad days, like when his father wouldn't co-sign, I'd find him curled into a fetal position, a pattern of behaviour that continued throughout the marriage. In the beginning, I tried to get him up. In time, I found that using the "tough love" approach exhibited by my dad was effective. "Give your head a shake. Look at our beautiful house and your family and get off the fucking floor," I'd say. It wasn't the right thing to do but that's how I'd deal with it, borrowing behaviour ingrained from childhood.

Other times, George's reactions would be violent. He did not touch me. Instead, I would hear him throw things at walls in a rage. Once, he ruined an antique chair. There were many times when he'd punch a hole in the wall. Once, I went for a run with my brother instead of him. George blew up after I got back home, and I left the house with John, terrified. My sister picked us up and we stayed with her for the day. I phoned the therapist I was seeing at the time and told her what had happened. She asked what I had done to provoke him. I hung up, feeling responsible, and returned home that night.

I had started therapy that same year, at George's suggestion. The reason why we weren't getting along was because of my childhood, he would say, and that I was the one who needed help. I was open to the idea, although I felt shame at first in admitting to people that I was talking to a professional. But, in time, I found that simply having someone listen to me was incredibly helpful in dealing with my anxiety. Things didn't seem so catastrophic.

That said, therapy didn't seem to solve anything. I'd ask pointed questions, wanting concrete answers to guide me. Do all relationships look like this? How many fights a week is normal? Should I keep a record of the number of fights and then average them out over a year and, if it is over a certain number, declare us unhealthy? How long do I hold out until I ask for a divorce? These things were left for me to decide but I had no idea how to think about them, or act.

George came to about three sessions, and they were filled with tension. His appearances came to an abrupt end after the therapist challenged George about his lack of trust and his jealousy toward me, which could be extreme, regardless of how many other women he had in his life. "Go fuck yourself," he told her and walked out of the office.

This was 1995, when the O.J. Simpson murder trial was in headlines, along with the subject of spousal violence. Photographs of Nicole Brown Simpson's beaten and bruised face taken by the Los Angeles Police Department were on the news repeatedly. Like everyone else, I watched the trial. Not once did I associate what was going on in my life with the abuse

Nicole experienced. I wasn't a "battered woman." Again, George didn't hit me, and I equated abuse with physical violence. We've since come to accept a broader definition of abuse that includes belittling, controlling and coercive behaviour, continual verbal insults and bullying, but that's not how I understood abuse at the time, and I'm not sure I was different from most women.

The only hint I had at that point in our lives that George could physically attack a woman came shortly after John was born. George's ex-fiancée, who'd broken off the engagement, threatened to sue him for abuse during the relationship. Exactly what had happened wasn't clear. He said he hadn't abused her and I encouraged him to fight it.

By this point, drinking to excess was becoming normal for George. Binge drinking is part of student life, but binge drinking and extreme behaviour are also hardwired into the "work hard, play hard" culture of the brokerage industry. It wasn't just normalized at Peters & Co., it was encouraged. Deals were done in bars. Business relationships were forged over drinks.

George would come home with wild stories about the brokerage industry. A broker George knew, a former athlete, filled his coffee cup with Jack Daniels and showed pictures of his sexual activities, which included swinging, to colleagues. According to George, a prostitute had been hired to sit all day in a cab in Toronto and give traders blowjobs during their breaks. Another acquaintance of George's spent $35,000 a month at Cowboys, a hot Calgary nightclub that seemed to specialize in busty serving staff. New hires were apparently encouraged to chew tobacco and drink caffeine all day long; the idea was that a completely wired employee was a better employee. Brokerages, from what I could see, were frat houses with money.

Some stories from this time were awful, some were funny. Once, when John was a baby, George came home during the Calgary Stampede—an annual week-long rodeo, exhibition, and festival that usually involves a lot of drinking—and headed to bed drunk. He woke up wearing his company's Stampede t-shirt, which read, "Think single, drink double, see triple." I was feeding John. It was dinner time. George read the clock wrong, thinking it was 6 a.m. and the markets were about to open on the east coast. He jumped in the shower and rushed madly out the door, twelve hours early. I let him.

Another time, George's co-workers brought him home, passed out, and put him on the front lawn. I came outside and turned the garden hose on him to wash his vomit off his pants. He still didn't wake up.

"Where do you want him?" his colleagues asked. I told them to take him upstairs.

When George woke up, he was apologetic. I saw that he felt guilty.

"Everything okay?" I asked.

Finally, he told me that'd he urinated on himself.

"Really?" I said. I didn't correct his mistake. I wanted him to be ashamed of his behaviour.

Of course, I contributed to the dysfunction. Early on, George and I drank together, and got drunk together. It would be fun until it wasn't. The wake-up call for me came after a night we'd gone out together, shortly after John was born. We'd wanted some fun. We got wasted, which was completely irresponsible, and I was still nursing. When we returned home, George's mother, who was babysitting, was furious, and rightly so. She stayed over that night because she didn't trust us.

Later, his parents sat us down and gave us a stern lecture, even after we'd apologized. "You can't do this stuff," they said, adding, "Don't worry, your secret is safe with us. Don't tell anyone and we won't either." George's whole family liked to keep problems under wraps.

1995 was also the year that I asked George to stop drinking. My mother had stopped, although she could still have a glass of wine here or there without any problem. He agreed and went to Alcoholics Anonymous a couple of times before abruptly quitting, saying that he couldn't identify with people who drank vodka in the morning and kept going all day.

"That's not me," he said. "I'm not that much of a drunk. I just need to control it."

"So control it," I said.

He abstained for almost a year. Then he began developing an appreciation for wine, and had the odd drink before dinner. I didn't complain. The truth was I liked it better when George had a couple of glasses of wine in the evening. It made him relax and open up. He'd listen to me and share details about his day. I felt I had his full attention, and George was fascinating to talk to when you got him on a topic that he knew a lot about, and fun or silly on a lot of other things. I liked to hear his take on the news, and to challenge him or try to impress him with my read on things. I enjoyed it when he took the time to help me understand something. Over time, however, the fact he only opened up to me with liquor became something I resented.

When John was about a year and a half old, we went to Club Med in Cancun: our first holiday away—just the two of us—since we'd become parents. I remember one time that we were at the beach and, as I was coming back from the washroom, I watched George hit on some woman, a scenario that played out a lot during the marriage. I returned to the hotel room. He followed and turned on me. He was livid and started to throw things. Then he moved toward me, but didn't touch me.

It was the first time George used John as leverage. "If you fucking think you're going to see your kid, if you think you can take him away from me, I will destroy your life," he told me, threatening to hire the best lawyers. "I will do anything and everything for you never to see your child, and I know how much you love that child." I had never threatened to leave him.

If George's goal was to scare the hell out of me, it worked. I didn't care in that moment that he'd intimated he would get physically violent. The idea of losing John was devastating. I imagined my beautiful baby boy being caught in the middle as George raged against me. *He means it*, I thought. I knew that if it came to fighting it out in court, George would win. He had the money and the control. I had heard those kinds of stories from other women; now I could see myself in one of them.

Whenever George threatened me in this way, I would have the same reaction. I could hardly breathe. My mouth would go dry, I wouldn't be able to speak, I couldn't think rationally. I was totally locked in fear, and I couldn't escape from that state until George said it was okay. I needed him to say, "Don't worry about it, it will be better. I'm sorry for what happened," and when I heard him say it, I would be fine. The resolution, when it happened, was almost like a drug. That dynamic of up and down, or threat and release, was a regular one in our relationship.

CHAPTER FOUR

Moving Up

GEORGE WANTED A SECOND CHILD and I began thinking it would be a good idea, too. We were fighting less and getting better at parenting. Having another child was the natural next step. George was thriving professionally and we had begun to look for a bigger house.

One day in 1997, George called with big news: "I bought us a house in Elbow Park," he announced, referring to a ritzy community in the southwest of the city. It was a red-brick Georgian. I'd toured it once along with some other houses, and had short-listed it as one of three houses for George to view. He'd toured the houses, liked the Georgian, and bought it immediately. It was a pattern: every house we owned, George bought without asking me first. I told a friend and she was amazed: "Are you kidding me? He didn't tell you? I would be so mad."

Our second house was a move up for us, but there were aspects of it that George hated. It was near a busy road, which could be loud. It was dark inside, too, which we both disliked. We fought over window coverings, even though that was my area of expertise. When we went to the store with a book of ideas I'd been collecting, I found he'd ripped out the page that featured ideas he didn't like. He told me I didn't know what I was talking about, and that we needed to hire a designer, never mind that I'd been trained as one. At the same time, I was also helping his mother with the window coverings in her home. Both of them would challenge everything I did.

I consulted my therapist about the situation. She told me that if I didn't want to stress about it, I should hand the projects over to George and his mother and profusely commend them on what a good job they did, because that is what they wanted to hear. I did exactly that and ended up with window coverings in our new house that I didn't like, just to avoid conflict.

In reality, home decor was just another thing for George to control. Every decision I made had to be approved by him: pillows, cutlery, furniture. The first time we traveled to New York, he took me to the china section in Bergdorf Goodman and told me to select all our fine china and silver place settings. I chose the patterns I liked. He was appalled by my choices and began picking out things he preferred. By this time, sensing the tension between us, the store clerk had gone off to help another customer. George then stormed off, mad at me and the lack of customer service.

We later wandered into a Calvin Klein home decor store and bought everything there: cutlery, place settings, linens, sheets, duvets—everything. We needed to buy a couple of extra suitcases to help us haul everything back. The place settings were particularly important to George. He was obsessed with plates, bowls, and good-quality drinking glasses, and would replace them every couple of years. In fact, he'd replace everything in the house every couple of years: mattresses, sofas, phones, cameras, bikes, cars, pots and pans, coffee makers, any fancy kitchen utensil. To him, almost every possession we had was just waiting to be upgraded when the new models were available.

I became pregnant in 1997, then miscarried at twelve weeks. Within months, I conceived again and, in January 1998, Carter was born.

Five days later, on a Saturday morning, we scrambled to take John and the baby skating in Stanley Park, where George's colleagues took their kids to play shinny. His parents came along. As I was lacing up John's skates, George had a public meltdown, behaviour I'd come to call the "Gosbee Show." His insecurity had begun to flare because he didn't skate as well as the others.

The same competitive streak that served George well in business could be trying to live with. George needed to be the focus of any room he was in. If people liked me more, it annoyed him. If someone looked better, it pissed him off. If someone played the crowd better, he'd have a problem with that person. If someone had more success or money, he was intimidated. And if they could skate well and he couldn't, he threw a tantrum.

He wanted to leave the rink. I could see John watching the other kids and wanting to stay, and I wanted to spend time with him after Carter's arrival so he didn't feel left out. At the same time, I was accustomed to stressful family relations in which the most difficult person takes everyone else hostage, so I let it happen. We trudged home and gathered around the fire. "I'm depressed," George announced. It was the first acknowledgement that he was dealing with mental illness. His mother and father were supportive. "We're so glad you're admitting that," they said. Everyone's focus was directed at getting George better.

A psychiatrist diagnosed him with Attention Deficit Disorder (ADD) and told him he could modify his mood swings with medication, a classic ADD diagnosis in the 1990s. George was put on drugs and started doing better; his moods stabilized. But he also harboured a fear that the medications would dampen his drive and undermine his success at a time when he was also going through a lot of professional changes. He was planning to launch his own business. If his extreme highs and lows were stabilized, he worried, would he be the same business genius?

George's concerns weren't misplaced. Business culture, and the investment industry especially, venerates winners, high-octane performers, and risk-taking alpha dogs. Admitting vulnerability or weakness isn't an option. Corner offices are often occupied by people with narcissistic, even sociopathic tendencies. The culture rewards it. That said, the same dominating, uncompromising, narcissistic traits admired in business can be hell on families.

Now that he had admitted his depression, all of us, including George's father, were expecting the drugs to magically take his problems away. But George was so worried about deleterious effects on his performance that he only took the medication for a half year, at most. He complicated the situation by drinking a lot while on the medication.

My night terrors continued, and my snoring or getting up to tend to the boys in the night would wake George. Eventually, I put a mattress in the boys' room so I could sleep there and avoid further conflict. I began to keep a journal to track my thoughts, often writing in the bathroom at night. Carter's birth had left me with some post-partum depression, and I felt overloaded trying to be a good mother to two boys and a wife to George. He would often say that he'd told me something that I honestly didn't remember. He'd say I was dumb. Keeping notes was a way of nailing down reality, making sure I wasn't going crazy.

Writing in my journal was the only outlet I had in my life that was mine alone. Or, so I thought at the outset. In fact, I didn't have any privacy. I'd find George had ripped pages out of the journal. He'd later show up to therapy sessions waving them as evidence of something he faulted me for. One therapist called him on it and told him I needed my own space. "Fuck off," he told her. We stopped going to that therapist.

Not long after Carter's birth, we traveled with George to New York City. While there, we replaced the wedding rings we exchanged in Turkey with more expensive ones. The French phrase *Pas moi sans toi* was inscribed on them, along with its English translation: *Not me without you*. It's a common romantic sentiment, the idea that one person isn't complete without the other. It also described the unhealthy degree to which I relied upon George for approval and identity, but I wouldn't see that for years.

CHAPTER FIVE

Success

I N 1997, GEORGE QUIT PETERS & CO. and went to work as managing director at Newcrest Capital, a Toronto-based brokerage that wanted a Calgary presence. Three years later, he did his own thing and founded G Capital, an investment firm that financed private-equity deals in the oil patch. Two years after that, he would roll G Capital into Tristone Capital, an energy firm involved in investment banking, property acquisition, and divestitures. He structured it in an innovative way that won him a lot of praise: he hired geologists and engineers to provide oil and gas expertise to the financial team, something that hadn't been done before.

George's success at such a young age was isolating for us as a couple. We were in our late twenties, but most people our age were going camping with their kids. That wasn't the type of holiday George wanted—he wasn't big on roughing it. He wanted to spend his money in ways that most people our age couldn't imagine. There was one couple our age with similar means and a child, and we spent time with them. That friendship came to an end, however, when George and the wife locked horns. I would lose a lot of girlfriends over the years because they didn't like being around George.

This left me without a lot of people other than George or my family to talk with. When John was about three years old, he asked, "Can we go see all your friends today?" It took me a while to realize he meant the people I conversed with regularly at Starbucks and Safeway. I joked about it at the time, but he was bang-on about who my friends were. In time, we fell in with a crowd who worked in George's industry but were a decade older. I'd forge solid friendships with some of the women, all the "Real Housewives" who stayed home with their kids.

It was around this time that George's violent outbursts started to occur more regularly. Once again, he blew up when I said I was going running with my brother. He thought I was saying he wasn't a good enough a runner to keep up. He took a hockey stick and started hacking at the branches of a pine tree in the backyard while yelling at the top of his voice. When I returned from the run, he exploded again on the driveway.

As things were breaking down with George, my relationship with my older sister Kathy, who also lived in Calgary, also became rocky. We were having difficulties, as sisters sometimes do, and George seemed to enjoy it. It proved to his satisfaction that my family did not appreciate me—that he was the only one who did. Unfortunately, the fracturing of my relationship with Kathy left me completely isolated. She was my go-to when George erupted and, as his drinking once again got worse and worse, he was erupting more and more. I felt like my only lifeline was being pulled away.

The part of our marriage that seemed to work best and be somewhat insulated from the tensions in our relationship was parenting. We were doing well with the two boys and by 2001 I was pregnant again, and hoping for a girl.

A week before our daughter, Isla, was born, my doctor told me that my blood pressure was dangerously high, and ordered me on bedrest. "I can't be on bedrest," I told her, explaining that George had an important client visiting from England. I was expected to host a dinner, and George would not accept that the needs of his wife and unborn child were an obstacle to that. My pregnancies simultaneously increased his need for control and his weird indifference towards me. My doctor looked at me with bewilderment. "Don't you get it?" she asked. "Your health is at stake. Hire a caterer." But my mind didn't work that way. My worry was that George would view hiring a caterer as a cop-out: "He will be so upset."

When I had John, my first-born, George had been high maintenance in the hospital, telling everyone he was always tense in hospitals because of his brain surgery. He complained he was nauseous. Finally, he fell asleep beside me—after he'd been given some meds to calm him down. I remember thinking, *I'm going to have this baby really quietly so I won't disturb him.*

The nurse had come in and asked, "How are you doing?"

"Okay," I told her. She checked and told me the baby's head was crowning. "You need to start pushing," she said. I knew I was ready to push. I was just trying to figure out how to do so without awakening the "Gosbee Show."

Isla's birth was the most difficult, and longest, labour I had. I had asked my mother to be in the delivery room for Isla's birth, as she hadn't witnessed the previous two. George wasn't happy about that either, and when he came around he accused me of paying more attention to my mom than to him. "I can't help but think you were really rude and you paid way more attention to your mother," he said while I was literally pushing my child out. *I can't believe this*, I thought. *Even during birth I'm not doing this right.*

I can see how strange the situation must look, but that was the "Gosbee Show."

Isla was born in July 2001, a week before the Calgary Stampede. When the event started, George went out and "stampeded," as they call all the drinking and partying that goes on, for the entire week.[3] One night, he was angry about something. He took the long-stemmed roses he'd sent me after Isla's birth out of a vase and swung them at me like a baseball bat, a baseball bat with thorns. Terrified, I had to get myself and the children out of there.

I gathered the kids and hustled them into the car and drove to a vacation home we'd recently bought a couple hours west of Calgary, in the Rocky Mountains. I had acted so quickly that none of us were wearing shoes. I have a vivid memory of walking through a mountain town while pushing a baby cart, carrying Carter, and holding onto John's hand, all of us shoeless.

---

3 There is a statistically significant connection between higher rates of domestic violence and certain events in Calgary: one being Calgary Stampeders' football games, the other being the Calgary Stampede. See Sophia Boutelier, et al., "The Connection between Professional Sporting Events, Holidays, and Domestic Violence in Calgary, Alberta," University of Calgary School of Public Policy Publications 10, no. 12 (June 2017). https://doi.org/10.11575/sppp.v10i0.42627

I walked down an alley so no one would notice us before I could buy some new footwear.

At the time, John, who was a solid sleeper, was still being night trained. While nursing Isla and tending to Carter's fears, I carried John to the toilet to go to the washroom. He dozed off on the toilet and then tried to crawl into the bathtub to sleep. After this had happened about three times, I lost it and yelled at him. It was all the pent-up anger I hadn't directed to George.

To this day, I feel immense guilt about it. I don't believe there's any good reason to raise your voice at a child beyond trying to protect them from harm. The only good thing that came of it was that John was suddenly night trained.

The whole summer of Isla's birth was tumultuous. George and I were fighting a lot, and he was now threatening to hit me when things escalated. One night he pushed me, and I fell and hit the side of my face on a chair. The next day I had to meet with his mom and his aunt. I remember sitting by a window in Starbucks, boasting a fresh purple bruise on my cheek, his mom looking at me. I never said a word about it and no one asked what had happened.

Why not leave him? It was complicated. After we fought, George would be apologetic and, again, I had a high tolerance—almost an expectation—of drama and trauma. Also, after Isla's birth, George became more involved with child-rearing. He was good at it, and she was an incredibly happy, sweet girl. She woke us up in the morning with a cheerful "Good morning, Mommy! How are you guys today?" She was so relentlessly sunny that George and I could hardly believe it. Between us, we gave her the ironic nickname "little bitch."

CHAPTER SIX

Trophy Life

I DISLIKE THE TERM "TROPHY WIFE." It reduces women to status objects, attractive accessories to "successful" husbands. But, in retrospect, I see how I internalized the role over time. By continually berating my intelligence and abilities, by always letting me know that I was not performing to his exacting standards, George reinforced the notion that my major contribution to our lives was to ensure that the Gosbees showed well.

It was a compulsion for him that everything look perfect and be in its place. Early on, shortly after Carter was born, he decided my housekeeping wasn't up to what he called "his level," and we hired our first housekeeper. Initially, he let me cook but was critical of my efforts, once writing with a Sharpie on a chili recipe I had used, "If you're going to make this fucking recipe, make it right." He expected me to have dinner ready for him every night when he arrived home—as far as he was concerned, it was my one responsibility during the day. During one of our visits to therapy, he was taken to task by the therapist, who told him, "If you want this marriage to work, either you learn how to cook or you hire a cook."

To his credit, George took over our dinners, and he brought to it the same focus he applied to business. He became a talented cook. For him, making pasta meant making it from scratch. Or he'd go on a ramen kick. It gave him another realm to dominate: when he cooked, I couldn't come into the kitchen. He also tended to make ridiculous amounts of food, like platters full of lamb and smoked meat. And we ate it.

I appreciate that George reinforced the importance of family dinner, something his parents had done. It was never a big deal in my house: in fact, we never ate together. George and I instead would always wait for the last child to be finished with his or her activities, whether hockey, dance class, or homework, and eat as a family. We have many good memories sitting around the dinner table.

It was also important to George that our homes be continuously renovated. When we did the mountain house in 2005, he gave me free rein to pick paint colors, kitchen cupboards, and floor finishes, while he approved the spending. He'd compliment me profusely about what I'd done and then point out to me how he'd complimented me profusely in front of other people. This was done to counter my arguments that he didn't trust my abilities as a designer, and that he was always putting me down. My work on the mountain house became his favourite example, when we fought, of his support for me. I was quite sure he let me do the mountain house because of the pressure he'd come under in therapy, and because he was spending a ton of money on a designer for our Calgary home. He was momentarily trying to save cash, but would never admit that to anyone.

When we went out, George liked me to style a look that he considered expensive and sexy, and which I viewed as somewhat slutty. I'm at home in jeans and a t-shirt or a cozy sweater. He liked me to show off my legs, so no long skirts. He despised patterns; couldn't handle them. To this day, I avoid patterns. He preferred no nail polish on my fingernails but liked fire-engine red on my toenails. I'm not sure where it came from, but he also had an obsession with Christian Louboutins, the ultra-expensive shoes with red soles, paired only with a white button-up shirt.

George's fashion instructions clashed with my efforts to develop my own style. When brown was trendy in 1994, I bought a leather coat at Banana Republic in New York City. "That's the ugliest thing I have ever seen," he said. "Take it back." I stood my ground and wore it. The funny part was that, a year later, he went out and bought an almost identical leather coat.

As George became more successful in the early 2000s, with Tristone handling big international deals, I increasingly became a measure and extension of his success. The wife of one of his partners once took him to task because I didn't have the latest bag or shoes. She questioned how successful the company could be if I didn't look the part. After that, George saw to it that the money I spent reflected on him. He also controlled our finances and dealt with our bankers, but gave me freedom to spend up to $2,000 per month for myself without his approval. I was never a big spender, although I understand that's relative. I could never wrap my mind around the idea of spending a thousand plus dollars or more on a purse every season, as many women I knew did.

Of course, I did appreciate our lifestyle and having nice things. I recognized the prestige that came with the clothes and jewelry. I rationalized that my circumstances weren't that bad, considering everything I was experiencing in my life. I was grateful to travel with the family, see different cultures and beautiful cities, and stay in luxurious hotels. There were restaurants, food, and expensive wine. Being married to George afforded many fine things that most people don't have the opportunity to experience. At the same time, I was acutely aware that I was deceptively privileged. From the outside it looked fantastic; inside, it felt rather empty.

When we shopped together, we shopped for him. I'd pick up things for myself by adding them onto George's order in the last ten minutes of being in the store. He didn't have the patience to let me leisurely look around, try something on and then decide. He also would occasionally buy me unscheduled gifts. Prada bags were a guilt gift from him, in return for abuse or what I later came to understand was misbehaviour on business trips.

We hired a nanny so I could travel with George when he wanted to show me off. He began pressuring me to have breast augmentation surgery, something I resisted as I didn't want big boobs. I'd always been flat-chested. After childbirth and nursing, however, my breasts looked like a quarter cup of soup in a bag. I finally agreed to see a specialist in 2003, after Isla was born. "Can you fix and lift?" I asked, but they told me instead that I needed saline implants. "You have no fat in your body and no boobs to correct," they explained. So I agreed to very small implants.

My reluctance to delve into plastic surgery made me an anomaly in the social circles where we traveled. Women I knew started using Botox in their twenties. Culturally, we were riding the first wave of the expressionless, synthetic, non-wrinkled face. We were pumped up and void of emotion. The younger women applied the same methods to their asses and hips; the older women wore the mask now familiar among the affluent, complete with chipmunk cheeks and frozen Daffy Duck lips—the face-caught-in-a-wind-tunnel look.

Everyone watched and took lessons from the Real Housewives of wherever. Anything TMZ exposed about the lifestyles of the rich and famous was duly noted. Our gathering places were coffee shops after our morning exercise or yoga classes. We talked about whatever entertained us at the moment. Exclusive gym and country club memberships allowed us the reassurance of being among other women who shared the luxury of "choosing" not to work, foregoing self-development and career ambitions to focus on raising children and building a family in a big, beautiful house with nannies.

I reminded myself often how many people would kill to have the same opportunities. I was in great physical shape, despite not having my own sense of purpose, but I was lonely. I couldn't have a sincere conversation with my peers. No one had privacy in these circles; information traveled fast, and was frequently embellished. There was not much real empathy, and not much support. In place of real community, everyone had a strong, isolated sense of her well-manicured self.

George, however, fit right in with this crowd. He was always super attentive to his own appearance, working out and taking HGH to bulk up. Over the course of our marriage he had Botox injections, regular spray tans, and two rounds of hair plug surgery. He considered this the price men paid to stay in a business that loved Young Turks.

The men also stayed young, or tried to, by partying like frat boys. One of George's former colleagues chartered a plane, filled it with staff from Cowboys, and took off for Las Vegas. Some of the men designed their homes around their fantasies: one had a glass shower installed within view of his bed so the action could be followed from one location to the other. Someone who cleaned up after some of the bigger parties in our community—huge affairs with DJs flying in from L.A.—said that the clean-ups involved throwing out all the couches, duvets, and carpets with wine, food, or human excrement stains, and replacing them. After closing big deals, it was customary in George's set to charter a plane and travel with the key people involved to a major sporting event for a "boys' getaway." I would later learn that mistresses or hired women were sometimes in attendance at these events, and that the plane was filled on its return with purchases paid for by their grateful hosts.

George, like most of the men he worked with, was obsessed with sports and would find any reason to attend a finals game or collect paraphernalia. His corner office was designed to display his collection of bats, baseballs, helmets, basketballs, hockey sticks, and framed jerseys, each signed by a sports legend or signifying a particular moment.

He was also obsessed with watches, as so many men are in the financial community. George was given a Rolex by his father when he graduated from university. He bought another Rolex to wear with casual attire. On one family trip to New York, he treated himself to a Franck Muller watch and had all the kids chanting "today is Daddy's day, today is Daddy's day, he deserves a gift today." Maybe I was tired, but I did wonder what distinguished Daddy's day from every other day.

George knew that he had only scratched the surface of the luxury watch world. He told me that, when he had more money, he would buy himself more expensive watches and a Bentley. In the meantime, he saw himself as sacrificing his material ambitions to provide for the family by "making do" with fakes.

George was introduced to the world of fake luxury watches on a trip to China in 2010, and went crazy buying replicas of all the brands he could not afford. Unfortunately, he was called out on one of his shooting trips for having a fake Patek Philippe 5270P Chronograph (the real thing retails for $192,780). An oil executive explained that the mechanics of George's watch were not real, that the date should show the month as well as the day, and that the face size was a little larger than normal. George was embarrassed and somehow, when he came home, it became my fault. It didn't stop him from buying the fakes, however. He refreshed his large counterfeit collection on later trips to China, although he only did so with mid-luxury watches: not the high-end variety, where the differences were easier to spot.

CHAPTER SEVEN

The Flood

W E MOVED HOUSE AGAIN IN 2004, this time only blocks away from the red-brick Georgian that we both hated. The new house was a showplace—modern, airy, and spacious, with a wall of windows overlooking a yard that rolled down to the Elbow River. George had kept his eye on it for a while. When a friend told me the owner was thinking of selling, George contacted him directly, toured it, and bought it privately on the spot for $3.2 million. Again, it was all his decision.

The Gosbee family may have appeared increasingly prosperous on the outside, but it remained impoverished within. After Isla was born in 2001, I was approached by a number of people who reported that George was cheating on me. I ignored them, questioning their motives. One person who told me this was my sister, Kathy, who, as I've mentioned, had a tense relationship with George. In turn, he often told me she hit on him. He knew my insecurities.

I confronted George about infidelity for the first time in 2002, after hearing repeatedly that he was involved with a woman I'll call DC. I was told he'd been seen all over Calgary with her. She was known for hanging out with a group of girls who held a "book club," a front for meeting new men and perhaps upgrading their partners. To get the men's attention, they would flirt and make out with each other in public. At a time (and in a city) where displays of same-sex affection were rare, it never failed to turn heads. George, at least while talking to me, referred to these women as the "town planks."

So many people warned me about DC that I couldn't ignore them. One day, I phoned George at work and asked him to come home, telling him it was urgent.

As I was hanging up the phone, his sister popped over to the house and caught the tail end of the emotional mayhem. "Is everything okay?" she asked. I told her I'd heard George was having an affair and that I wanted to clear it up with him.

"I always thought it would be you," she said as she turned to leave. I was dumbfounded, but I was more concerned with how to handle George.

When he arrived, I said, "I hear you're having this affair. Talk to me."

He denied it. I told him I was not happy with the marriage, and was trying everything I could to make it better. I demanded he call DC on speaker phone, with me in the room, and tell her that we had heard rumors, and he wanted her to stop saying there was something between them; that he was committed to his wife and to working on his marriage.

George agreed and dialed the number. DC saw George's name on call display and answered with a breathy "Hi, George." George was all business: "Hey, D. It's George Gosbee. I'm sitting here with my wife."

"Oh," she said.

He told her what I said.

"You both are crazy, fuck you both!" she screamed, and hung up. She was right. I was being crazy, and that was not solving my problems. George and I looked at one another and burst out laughing. The survival humour was kicking in.

George saw his opening: "Karen, I love you so much, I would never do that." He called DC a "town plank" again, and said she wasn't his type: "She's way too big for me." He thought body-shaming her was a way to reassure me. I knew he was covering for something, but by then I craved the feeling of being calm and settled. I wanted at least momentary relief from my state of panic about what might happen next.

George kept on having affairs and I went into denial, which was difficult to sustain when I found earrings in his car that weren't mine. George made it easy to figure out who he was seeing, though. He would get "mention-itis," and talk a lot about women he was interacting with: a trainer, a restaurant hostess, an investment banker, our private banker, a realtor. Then he'd suggest I become friends with them. "You should meet so-and-so," he'd say. "She's really nice. You'd like her." If he was very involved, he would mention them during sex, as if in his imagination they were joining us during our love making. He'd plead for me to have a threesome, which I refused.

An older woman I looked up to told me once that there was no escaping the threat of women circling our husbands. You will get older, she said, and their age will remain the same. Our lifestyle will always be very attractive to people who don't share it. She tried to comfort me: "At least he'll always come home to you."

It wasn't much comfort, especially when I heard of groups of girls who kept black books on how much each man earned, if his marriage was solid, and if there was potential for a monetary arrangement: in other words, if he would he make a good "sugar daddy." Some of these women worked in the industry as brokers or assistants. Some of them were just on the prowl.

* * *

We settled into the new house in 2004, which remained largely unfurnished because we couldn't agree on anything about decorating it other than we wanted it light and airy, with white walls. Finally, I suggested we hire a designer. I called him our "mediator," a peacemaker for the Gosbee household. I would learn that a lot of other couples we knew used designers in the same fashion.

The lack of furniture became an unexpected benefit when Calgary experienced unexpected and widespread flooding in June 2005. I looked out our bathroom window one morning to see people—volunteers, I'd later learn—putting sandbags around our house. Our neighbours, whose family had owned the property next door since 1928, were blasé: "Don't worry," they said. "It's not going to flood."

By nightfall, water from the Elbow River was pouring into our basement, forcing us to move out. I took the children to stay with friends for the night, while George stayed behind to keep watch. True to form, George rose to the occasion, and became a community leader.

The flood was devastating for many—including the affluent—because of a lack of available resources, but it also had unexpected benefits. It was a shared crisis, and it forged a strong community spirit. Everyone opened their homes, and family and friends came in to help. There was a sense of banding together in shared purpose, of solidarity that was truly comforting.

As I mentioned, we didn't have a houseful of furniture. But one object ruined in the flood, a painting, had symbolic importance to me. I'd purchased it at ArtRageous, an annual fundraising gala thrown by the Alberta College of Art and Design, where George was the board chair. We'd had a rocky day, fighting, and were at the gala with a couple who were close friends. We bought a ticket with a number that matched the number on an art piece produced by an ACAD alumnus. I loved the one we got, a moody yellow and black abstract reminiscent of the cover of Tracy Chapman's self-titled album, which had the hit "Fast Car."

Later, the artist called to thank me for supporting ArtRageous, and I asked her about the painting. She'd titled it "Rage," she told me, and it was part of a series she'd done after studying women in abused environments. I took a deep breath. "That's fitting," I told her. "That's what my life feels like right now." At the time, I understood George's behaviour as "rage." I didn't consider it abuse.

I now see the years after the flood, from 2006 to 2008, as the best years of our marriage. We established a nucleus of friends during the flood, people with kids the same age. We finally had a sense of community and connection with people of common interests. We'd hang out, travel, go to restaurants. Calgary was booming financially and that ushered in a vibrant arts scene and sense of optimism.

In a weird twist, I was approached to participate in a "Real Housewives of Calgary" show. I said "no" immediately, and I actually wanted to cry that I was even considered. George was all for it. He had no problem being in the spotlight. I did, but that's not why I rejected the idea.

I dislike the "Real Housewives" franchise for a number of reasons. First, I dislike the focus on petty grievances and women forming ugly rivalries, while the real problems are shoved under the carpet. It's something that mirrors too closely what happened in my childhood, and what was playing out in my life at that time. Even more, I dislike those shows because they normalize toxic behaviour. In the end, the Calgary "Real Housewives" show never got off the ground.

Publicly, George and I appeared to be in sync, even to the point of wearing matching Hermès "half-sun" necklaces. Together they formed a whole sun. George ordered them for Christmas 2005, after he saw Demi Moore and Ashton Kutcher wearing them in *People* magazine. The matching jewelry didn't help Demi and Ashton's marriage; they split up in 2011, just after their sixth wedding anniversary.

Over time, my behaviour outside the house increasingly accommodated George. I learned to hold back. He was often described as charismatic, and certainly he could be that when he was excited about something and when he wasn't drinking too much. But he still suffered from insecurity, and if he couldn't hold court or if there was someone he felt was equal to or better than him, he would shut down and become anti-social. When we went to go to school fundraisers, he could be like a shadow. It often made him jealous that I don't have a problem meeting people. "You forget I'm there," he'd complain. He'd get furious if he felt I was getting more attention, or more laughs. I learned to moderate my behaviour in groups, instead. Many times I'd say something funny to him, and he'd recycle my comments as if they were his.

I was asked to join the Calgary chapter of the Canadian Women's Foundation, a group devoted to empowering women and girls to move out of poverty and violent situations toward self-sufficiency and leadership positions. Its members tend to be affluent and well-networked women, which means they're in a great position to approach their peers to raise money for those in need. The women who founded the group modelled for me what you can do when you have a vision and want to make a difference. I was inspired by incredible people like JudyLynn Archer, who helped build Women Building Futures with its mandate to "empower women to succeed in non-traditional careers, inspiring positive economic change for women."

I was thrilled to be asked to join the women's foundation but explained that I wanted to be actively involved, by which I meant I wanted to do more than raise money. "You can mentor women in need," I was told. Hearing that made me want to burst out crying. The idea was that I would use my design skills to mentor women living in poverty or to help them decorate their own living quarters, something that my own husband didn't have confidence in me doing. But I felt I had nothing to offer; I didn't even have any knowledge about or access to my own financial situation.

The reality of my home life left me feeling remote from these women as we sat enjoying wine and cheese and mulling lists of potential donors on the deck of someone's indoor Olympic-sized pool on a freezing February evening. We were talking about women in need, and I was slowly beginning to realize I was one.

Even so, our home life was still better than usual during this period because George was happy. His business was thriving and his public profile was rising. He was spending more time on public causes, including fostering political engagement. We started hosting salon evenings that featured a politician or keynote speaker. During the provincial elections, we hosted Alberta's most important political leaders, including Ed Stelmach and his successor as premier, Alison Redford. On the federal level, Liberal leader Michael Ignatieff and Bank of Canada governor Mark Carney came to speak to our peers. I learned a lot from those evenings.

We still had fights, but they'd be spaced out—every three weeks or so. If I sensed George was going to be angry when he got home, I'd invite people over to deflect it.

When I look at pictures taken at the time, they're filled with a lot of socializing and heavy-duty drinking. Almost every weekend, someone was hosting a dinner or a much-anticipated party. There was a group of people open to drugs—maybe a toke, edibles, or a line of coke—and others that weren't. I wasn't drinking much and I was not open to drugs, but I would watch people come and go as they used, and see how their behaviours altered. They tended to become more arrogant, more flirtatious, and more confrontational. George couldn't mix alcohol and recreational drugs without becoming adversarial. When he did, I'd get dragged into disputes that he started. Or we would leave and he would start fighting with me.

I was often hyper-vigilant at these parties. One night after a dinner, I stepped outside and saw a couple who seemed happily married locked in conflict: he was raging at her in an ugly, mean way, and she was silently taking it. Up to that point, I couldn't figure out why she was so aloof in the group, or why she would sometimes say silly things; or seem angry, or high, or numb. This offered a clue. It also told me I wasn't alone.

In time, I became increasingly cynical about the value systems surrounding me. I struggled with my privileged lifestyle, the fact that I drove a new Range Rover and spent my days working out, meeting friends for coffee, and going from shopping to beauty appointments. I didn't find purpose in days divided between my children's activities and trying not to upset George. I worried about the effects of all this on the kids, and became more deliberate about teaching them that we were no different from anyone else, that all people are equal, and that we had far more privilege than most.

There was no question we were privileged. We had access to preferential medical treatment, for instance. In 2003, one of George's friends had visited a Scripps Clinic in California, where they found a latent pulmonary aneurysm that required urgent surgery. George got paranoid and immediately booked himself into the same clinic for a full-body check-up. We chartered a plane with another couple and flew to San Diego to have our physicals. After a day of intense probing and screening, it was decided we all needed to spend time in Vegas as a reward for our clean bills of health. We hopped on the plane and headed to Vegas.

It was not a great time. I was exhausted and did not want to go drinking and gambling. I wanted to rest and relax, and the whole trip felt like an overindulgence. Fortunately, we were all exhausted and, after a dinner, we went to bed at 10 p.m. George was embarrassed, and told me I had ruined the trip.

Where I got a real up-close look at wealth, and what it could do to wives, was during our annual hunting trips in England. George began shooting game birds in England after Isla was born. In time, I'd accompany him, although I didn't shoot. Very few women in the group did; it wasn't encouraged. We'd stay at beautiful old inns or castles in northern England and Scotland. The same men who participated in these excursions also took luxurious trips to trophy hunt in Africa, ticking off whatever exotic animal they needed on their hit lists.

The shoots in England were highly ritualistic. The shooters wore high cashmere socks, leather-lined rain boots, tattersall shirts, ties, vests, and flat caps. Each shooter had a matching pair of expensive shotguns that were managed by a loader. Beaters walked through the fields to rouse the birds, which would fly anywhere from twenty-five to a hundred yards above the shooters, who would then blast away. People with hunting dogs would pick up the dead birds and, as they did, the shooters were served sloe gin, champagne, and canapes. Lunch was an elegant affair served in a dining room with china and crystal, a three-course meal, and more alcohol. There was a bit more shooting after lunch, following which scores are tallied over tea and scones with clotted cream. Then everyone returned to quarters in Range Rovers and, after getting cleaned up, met again for cocktails in bespoke smoking jackets and velvet monogramed slippers. On it went into the evening.

As the years passed, I increasingly felt like I was a witness and not a participant during those trips to the U.K. I found myself watching for commonalities amongst the wives supporting these men. I started to notice the tells of who in the group was experiencing an abusive environment at home. These women all drank what was regarded as socially responsible amounts. Yet, by the end of the night, a handful would be completely numbed out—some combination of alcohol and prescription drugs would be my bet. That's how they were surviving.

One morning at breakfast, I sat with a woman who'd had so much cosmetic surgery that her face was expressionless. Even though it was first thing in the morning, she was all dolled up. I sat there, judging her. Then, as we started to speak, it became apparent we had a lot in common. She told me how difficult it was to buy a present for her husband: "He's never happy with what I get him," she said. The other women were trying to console her, and offer suggestions.

I can relate, I thought to myself. There were so many birthdays and Christmases when I'd failed to get the "right" gift for George and an argument would ensue. "Just put some thought into it," he'd say angrily, as though I hadn't been agonizing over it for the last three months. He would tell me how his assistant and parents were so good at giving gifts. All I had to do was pay attention, he said. It had reached the point where I'd actually panic when it came to special occasions.

As this woman continued talking, I made a mental checklist:

"You have no idea of how difficult it is to live with him," she said. Check.

"There's not a lot of people I can relate to. I have a hard time hanging out with family." Check.

"My only support is the family he has allowed me to be with." Check.

I was beginning to see: *Oh yeah, that's me too.*

Later, George and I would talk about the others and give pet names to the other couples, unkind behaviour that I now regret. It was my way of distancing myself, of seeing them as the "other" when in fact they were me, and that was my future. We tend to be most critical of people we see our own worst traits in.

I was fond of the woman at breakfast, who was the wife of an extremely wealthy and prominent Albertan. She confided to me that she'd written a book about her situation. I told her she should publish it. "There's no way I could do that," she said. I asked her where it was. She said no one knew.

I'd been keeping a journal for years but I became more deliberate about writing things down after that. You write it down because you have no one to talk with. You write it down because you want a record. You write it down because you want proof you exist. I was increasingly aware of how I was viewed as an extension of George. As he always told me, I'd be nothing without him.

That idea was reinforced by friends. I had been close to a woman whose husband worked for George, and was later let go. She told me she didn't respect me for being with George and severed our relationship. I was heartbroken. I had had a ton of fun with her, and shared a lot. We had talked every day. It wasn't the first time I had lost a friend because she couldn't take George, though. I became more guarded after that experience, and avoided getting close to people for fear of losing them.

While George was happier than usual during this period of our lives, it was nonetheless becoming clear to me was that no amount of wealth provides real, enduring happiness. And no amount of wealth was going to satisfy George. When we were first married, George said his goal was to make $3 million. Then he wanted to make $10 million; then $15 million. When he'd make it, I'd say, "Remember when you said, 'If I had $3 million, I'd be satisfied'?" But it was never enough. Then the goal was to make so much that George could retire when he turned forty in 2009. That used to terrify me. I didn't know what he would do if he retired.

Then it all became academic. The stock market crashed, and our lives with it.

CHAPTER EIGHT

The Crash

THERE ARE CERTAIN CONSTANTS ABOUT intimate-partner violence that apply whether you're rich or poor. For one, it gets a lot worse when there are financial pressures: job loss, debt, chronic unemployment. In 2015, there was a 40 percent uptick in reports of abuse after mass layoffs in the Alberta oil patch.[4] In my marriage, the financial crash of 2008 ushered in a new reign of terror.

The year began optimistically. George and his partners had decided to sell Tristone Capital, which they'd built into the world's largest independent oil-and gas-property acquisition business in less than six years.

By 2008, Tristone employed more than 160 people, with offices in Calgary, Houston, Denver, London, and Buenos Aires. They were fielding attractive offers, including one from the Australian company Macquarie Group, and others from the Middle East. Because September was the holy month of Ramadan that year, they couldn't negotiate with the Middle Eastern buyers until month's end. But on September 15, 2008, the powerful global financial services firm Lehman Brothers tanked, putting into motion a global economic crisis and throwing George into a dark spiral.

---

4 See CBC News, "Alberta economic woes drive up to 40% increase in domestic violence calls," October 27, 2015. https://www.cbc.ca/news/canada/calgary/domestic-violence-oil-patch-1.3291744

Between the market free fall and the partners not agreeing on the sale, it was constant doom and gloom at home. Tristone was facing major layoffs and might have to close offices. Every day the sky was falling, and while I had no responsibility for the global economy, somehow the fault was often mine.

George couldn't believe that his wealth—"my wealth," as he referred to it—had been more than halved. If we'd been worth $50 million—I never knew the exact figures –suddenly we were worth $20 million. I know that doesn't inspire sympathy, but after a while you can lose perspective as to what is significant and what isn't.

That was never more apparent than when we traveled to England for our annual shooting trip in October. Compared to the wealth of some of these guys, George and I were hired help. One head of a major international oil company was complaining that he had to give up one of his three jets. George had lost millions, but these guys had lost billions.

After the crash was when George began binge drinking daily. He'd easily go through two bottles of wine a night. I'd drink two glasses, max, but George would finish the bottle, then another, and start pouring Scotch. It wasn't uncommon for him to eat nothing during the day, and then doze off at the dinner table. The family was now on high alert, just as my family had been with my mother. The children all recall helping their father from the table to bed. We'd learn to look for signs that he was drinking at work, and figure out how to get him home safely.

Vodka became George's preferred drink because it wasn't as detectable. He'd pour it in empty water bottles that he'd leave around the house, in drawers, and jacket pockets. More than once, one of the kids would mistakenly take a swig out of one. I did, too.

George was also mixing vodka with the prescription sleeping drug Ambien, which would create a volatile situation. He was always more confrontational at those times. He'd blame his need for the pills on the amount of traveling he was doing, and having to adjust to new time zones. I found it easier than you might expect to adjust to his new habits. Finding drugs and alcohol hidden around the house also took me back my childhood.

It's said that alcoholism is a breaker of relationships, and that was true for us. Leaving aside the personal susceptibilities that had me tolerating more of his abuse than was wise, I'd always clung to the fact that George was a strong parent and that putting up with him was good for our family. George's drinking now made him an absentee parent. The kids learned not to expect him at their events: Isla's dance recitals, the boys' hockey games. John doesn't remember George being at any of his graduations or big moments. He has one memory of his father taping a hockey stick, before George got frustrated and asked me to do it.

The children also learned not to speak to their father about work because that only made him more stressed. The year before the crash, George had started experiencing panic attacks that sometimes landed him in the emergency room. And through it all, he was still injecting HGH, which worsened his rages.

The more George felt like a failure at work, the more he raged. He would get a sarcastic smile, as though he could envision how he was going to have some fun being mean. He locked me out of the house at night several times, forcing me to sleep in the car, and mocked me constantly, telling me that I was stupid. Whenever that happened, my response was always the same. Fear would hijack my body: my mind would go blank, my body temperature would drop, and I would start to shiver. I would feel my lips go dry, and lick them. Here George would mimic me, licking his lips too. He'd make fun of me stuttering and not being able to follow a train of thought, which discombobulated me even more.

This is a delicate detail but crucial to communicate just how profoundly emotional abuse can affect the body: when George and I were in conflict or when I was experiencing fear of what he would do, it registered directly in my bowels. I'd have to find a bathroom immediately. The amygdala is the part of the brain that's responsible for mediating our survival instincts, our emotions, and our memory. It typically works like a barking dog: it warns you when you're in danger. My barking dog is my bowels, and the response was always urgent. Even a look, or an angry text, could trigger the sensation. It was a singular response to the sense of fear George elicited in me. I never reacted in the same way to other anxiety-producing scenarios.

They say violence begets violence, and this was true of George. The more he did it, the more violent he became. His eyes would narrow, his jaw and neck would tense, and he'd puff his chest as if he was preparing to charge or hurt me. He was getting hostile to me in front of the kids. "I can't keep doing this, George, you are exhausting me," I'd tell him.

I have a high pain tolerance. When I was pregnant with Carter, my water broke and we were in the ER with people screaming around us. The nurse sent us away, explaining that I wasn't in distress and was just taking up space. George insisted she check me. When she did, they discovered I was fully dilated and ready to give birth. Carter was born ten minutes later, with no epidural. One therapist told me, "You're like a thoroughbred; you're like the only who could keep up with him." It sounds like a compliment but it's not. My ability to withstand pain without complaining allowed me to put up with far more than I should have.

Still, I believed our problems were fixable. I bought books, and asked George to go to couples counselling. He wasn't interested. Instead, he told me that if I could be a better wife—smarter, better organized—we wouldn't have all the conflict: "What the fuck, Karen . . . if you just tried a little harder. Do you know how hard I work for you to have all this?" It seemed lost on him that he wanted "all this" a lot more than the rest of us did.

George was functional at work, although he was going in later and later in the morning. He'd started missing work and canceling meetings for trivial reasons—because he was upset with his partners, because he didn't feel well, because he was upset at me, or just because he could. But he hung in and, towards the end of 2008, he bounced back. He was tapped to be the vice-chairman of the Alberta Investment Management Corporation (AIMCo.), a huge provincially run institutional pension fund that he'd helped found.

Around this same time, my own story took a turn that had ramifications for years to come.

CHAPTER NINE

Strayed

I TURNED FOR ADVICE to a skating coach I'd met through the boys' hockey activities. He twigged to the inequity in my relationship with George and presented himself as someone who cared, as someone who could help. He was a few years older than me (I was thirty-eight) and unmarried. I saw him as a good guy. He kidded around with me and the kids.

He was a heavy-duty flirt, but he was like that with all of the mothers. "If you ever want to hit me up," he'd joke. I thought he was cheesy, and I wasn't remotely interested, but I liked him. I won't say the flirting didn't make me feel good. It did. It was a relief to have someone engage with me, and flatter me, at a time I was being constantly berated at home.

A lot of men had told me over the years they were available for sex, usually married guys who were competitive with George. The world they came from was all about power, money, and ego. This guy wasn't of that world, and I found that refreshing. But an extramarital affair was the last thing on my mind, however common they were in our circle.

George constantly told me stories about colleagues who were sleeping around or engaged in swinging and S&M. A close friend of his had left his family once on Christmas Day and didn't show up again until after Boxing Day. It was assumed he'd gone to stay with the woman he was having an affair with.

I was friends with this man's wife and she came to ask me what I knew.

"Is he having an affair?" she asked.

"What do you plan to do with that information?" I asked her.

"I don't know," she said.

"When you have a plan, let me know, and we can talk," I told her. It was good advice. I could help other people but not myself.

I was under no illusions about George. In time, I'd learn that the all-guys trips he went on to Spain and to the 2006 Olympics in Turin often involved hiring women to "entertain." The atmosphere around his shooting gang reeked of testosterone. They didn't consider what they were doing to be cheating. It was just the "bro-hood." They were very loyal to one another, and the only way to learn of their activities was by accident—someone happened to see or hear something. A woman told me that one of the people George accompanied to Turin had a special woman with him the entire time. I asked George if this was true, and he told me he didn't know what I was talking about. That was the bro-hood.

They also had executive assistants who protected them. The assistants had one story for the wife and another for friends and mistresses. Most assistants in the banking world were bonused on their boss's performance. They would help in any way they could. They were usually physically appealing, if not provocative, and they gave good phone, as George described it. A good executive assistant would sense what the boss wanted at all times. That led to a lot of romances, and a surprising number of them ended up at the altar.

One day in 2009, after another fight and another night of being forced to sleep in my car, the hockey coach approached me after I'd dropped the boys off at tryouts. He saw I was frazzled, and grabbed me by the arm.

"What's up with you?" he asked.

"Nothing," I told him.

He didn't buy it: "No, I can tell something's up."

I didn't want to talk about it. That was how I coped.

"It's nothing," I said.

He refused to let it go.

"I know what's going on at home," he said. "If you ever want to talk about it, I'm here."

After I left, I just drove around because I didn't want other parents to see me upset. Going home wasn't an option because George was there and still furious with me, as was evident from the torrent of texts I was receiving. The coach called to check in: "Are you okay?" he asked. Just hearing that, I burst out crying. It was the first time in years I felt as if I had been seen. I spilled out everything that happened the previous night and told him I hadn't talked to George since being locked out.

"Give it time," he said. "Don't call him. You'll just aggravate him. Let him calm down and give it until noon."

From then on, he became my coach as well. He was kind, someone I could talk to. He understood family trauma, having been abused as a child, and also understood how to alleviate a crisis situation. After George had raged and drunk himself to sleep, I'd text X (as I'll call him) with George passed out next to me.

It wasn't quite is simple as that, of course. As all of this was happening, the coach was pushing my boundaries. Once, he texted me a photo of his penis (this was a few years before the Anthony Weiner scandal). I was grossed out and erased it immediately. I figured he was probably doing the same thing with four or five other women; anyone he thought might be receptive. *I don't need this*, I thought, but by then I did not want to lose him as a friend and coach.

George found out about my texting relationship with X when we were in Costa Rica in February 2009. My phone wasn't working and he was helping me connect to wifi. When he finally did, all of X's messages popped onto the screen, things like "Hey, I miss you."

"What's this?" George asked, holding up the phone.

I told him X was just a friend, which was technically true. After that, he demanded full access to my phone, and I agreed. In time I would learn this is called technological stalking. People who are suspicious of their partners and have the means to do so install spyware on computers and phones, put hidden cameras in the house, hack into their partner's social media and email accounts, or install GPS devices on vehicles.

In May 2009, Tristone was sold for $130 million. George had been having major friction with his partners, but he was back in the money. We took our annual family trip to celebrate Isla's birthday on July 6; that year, we went to Rome. It also didn't deter George from wanting an extended blowout to celebrate his fortieth birthday on August 30. He talked about chartering a boat and paying for our closest friends and their families to cruise around the Mediterranean or someplace warm.

Here I put my foot down. I refused to waste all that money. On the one hand, George always fretted about needing to buy friends; on the other, he was often the one footing the bill for group activities. I'd assure him that his friends liked him for himself, which I believed was true, although there was a part of George that always struggled to fit in—that made us compatible, in a way.

I organized my own surprise trip for George instead. First, I invited twenty friends to join us in the Napa and Sonoma regions before the grape harvest. Then I brought George to Frog's Leap Winery in Napa for a tour. At the end of the tour, all of our friends were waiting in a courtyard to join us for lunch. The surprise was followed by a weekend of activities to celebrate his birthday. Everyone I invited came, paying their own way. That gesture meant a lot to him. It probably wasn't the best way to discourage his drinking, but I was far more concerned with giving him a satisfactory fortieth birthday.

We celebrated George's birthday again on the actual day with a big party at the house. We had a band and Isla sang a song for her dad, who was drinking and high from some edibles that friends had brought. Around 10 p.m., when the party was in full swing, one of our friends came over to me. "You're not drinking at all, Karen," he said, grabbing my hand to lead me to the bar. George was watching and became so angry that he went to bed, leaving a hundred people in the garden celebrating his birthday.

A group of friends headed upstairs to try to rouse him; but it was normal George behaviour.

George was known for tantrums at work, and people indulged him; they saw it as part of the passion or drive that made him successful. (Earlier in our marriage, we'd had a party with his colleagues to celebrate a big deal. Something upset him, and he punched a hole in the wall with his fist before abandoning us and heading to bed.)

I was surprised that it was my actions at the party, not George's, that came under criticism. "What do you expect? You were holding hands with his close friend," I was told. I spent the rest of the night anxious, with my mouth dry and my ears unable to hear. I finally shut the party down at 4 a.m., long after I was ready for people to leave. The last person out the door was an ex-boyfriend. As we were talking, he told me how happy he was for me that I had a beautiful family and such a lovely life. There was a ton of irony in that.

The birthday celebration continued the entire year. I referred to it as "George's Centennial." (When he was in the right mood, I could tease him—pointing out, for instance, that his Prada man purse was undermining the masculine vibe he was otherwise striving for.) In October, he invited our core group of friends from the 2005 flood to come pheasant shooting with him in England. In photos, George is always in the middle. The group called him "The Prince," because if he didn't get his way, he'd throw a fit.

While the Tristone sale had improved George's finances, it left him at loose ends, without a full-time job. He wanted to be in the mix and make more money, but it wasn't happening.

He was still involved in public policy. The federal finance minister at the time, Jim Flaherty, tapped him in December 2008 to sit on the newly formed federal Economic Advisory Council to consult on the 2009 federal budget, and he'd even been approached to run for office. In July 2009, then-prime minister Stephen Harper supported his appointment to the board of Chrysler Group LLC, where he was to serve as a steward of the government's financial crisis bailout money. We'd been in Rome, the whole family sitting on the Spanish Steps eating gelato, when George first heard about the Chrysler board; it was a beautiful summer night, and he was in a great mood. I'll never forget that moment; he loved how much recognition the position would bring him. When the appointment was mentioned in the press, the stories invariably mentioned that George drove a Chrysler Dodge Ram pickup truck and a Porsche Cayenne SUV. "It's ironic," he told me. "I don't even own a Chrysler." I had to remind him that we did.

The Chrysler opportunity notwithstanding, George was unable to land enough board positions to support the lifestyle he wanted. So, in 2010, he created AltaCorp Capital Inc., an investment dealer tailored to the resource industry. It was an innovative company in that it focused not only on oil and gas production but on emerging technologies like agri-food and energy technology. George's negotiating finesse, and his charm, led to a deal with the Alberta government, then headed by Alison Redford, to partner AltaCorp with ATB Financial, an Alberta government-owned lender. That partnership gave AltaCorp considerable muscle for a small shop. George was very close to Redford and to Danielle Smith, leader of the Wildrose Party, who would do anything for George.

His support for the community and his desire to "give back" was sincere. He sat on numerous boards, including those of the Libin Cardiovascular Institute of Alberta and the Alberta Investment Management Corporation (AIMCo, and was vice-chair at the Alberta Economic Development Authority, and chairman of the School of Public Policy at the University of Calgary.

In the years his businesses did well, George was also generous with charity: the United Way, Right to Play, STARS air ambulance, and another emergency ambulance service were among the causes he supported. He could be awesome coming up with creative fundraising ideas. Once he suggested putting executives on mountain peaks; they would have to use their cell phones to raise money in order to be lifted off. George could also be very generous when his employees had addiction problems: a model other companies should follow. I know that he paid for rehab for three employees (two men and a woman); sadly, one of the men later died by suicide.

George's philanthropy definitely had a positive impact on me. To his credit, George encouraged me to get involved on boards and community work, for which I'm grateful. My first board involvement happened in 2009 after George stepped down from the board of Edge School, where our kids went, and he suggested I take his place. He also paved the way for me to sit on the board of the Calgary Philharmonic Orchestra, a wonderful experience that taught me how non-profit boards should be properly run. When George was angry, he would remind me he had done so and that, if it weren't for him, I'd never understand how boards are run or have the opportunity to sit on one because I was so fucking stupid. I heard that a lot.

The first board I sat on without George's input was for Classroom Champions, started by Olympian Steve Mesler and businessman Mark Fitzgerald. The program partners an Olympic athlete with a challenged classroom to teach the values of community, goalsetting, and discipline. However, I sensed that my involvement on its board threatened George. One day, he volunteered to help me with a fundraiser we were struggling with. He ended up staging the entire thing by organizing a panel of big-name hockey players who shared stories about how their mentors helped them achieve success. He helped us raise $200,000, an amount we'd never have raised during an economic downturn without his connections. I once overheard him talking on the phone to one of his colleagues: "Come on, I'm going to put you down for $20K. You spend more on that for hookers most weekends. This is going to help little kids."

At home, the fights continued, and were often witnessed by the children. As Isla was the youngest, she was the most vulnerable, a realization that chills me today. One night in 2009, when Isla was in fifth grade, George began calling me names in a low voice after I told him I didn't want to fight. "I'm not fighting, I'm whispering," he told me. I locked myself in the bathroom, my usual retreat. Isla woke up and knocked on the door, and said she would sit beside me. Together, we waited for George to pass out. I knew that if I waited long enough, he would eventually fall into a drunken stupor and we'd have our chance to tiptoe back to bed.

Another time, George had passed out while laying half on Isla's blanket and half off of it. Isla needed her blanket, and I pulled it out from under him quickly so as not to wake him; it didn't work. He stood up and exploded at me, while Isla was by my side. "I want to fight," he said, so we went downstairs before he finally chased me out of the house. His chasing me out of the house happened four or five times. I'd end up just driving around, wondering how the kids were, feeling like such a loser. I didn't want to check into a hotel because I knew I wouldn't sleep for worrying about the children.

As I drove, I was a mess physically, freezing and thirsty and needing to go to the washroom. Mentally, I wouldn't feel better without some kind of emotional resolution with George, but I knew I couldn't go home for six to eight hours—enough time for him to calm down. Otherwise, he'd chase me out again.

The result of these explosions was a fear-based home. We were always walking on eggshells. Of the three children, Carter was the one often caught in the middle. My middle child had a complicated relationship with his father; as a baby, he'd squirm when George held him. He always intuitively knew if I was upset and was very protective of me, and has grown up to be that way with anyone he adores. Carter missed nothing when it came to his father's actions.

At the time, I gave George credit for never being violent or abusive with the children—it was directed at just me. (Just me.) That doesn't mean that his behaviour, or the way I dealt with it, didn't hurt them. Any parent who uses violence or neglect towards their partner is neither a good parent nor a role model.

Because the kids were scared, they often slept together. They also wanted to be near me to protect me. When Isla was seven, she slept in our room in a little bed. There are two philosophical approaches to dealing with children with sleep issues: you can night parent, or be hardcore militant by putting them down and leaving them until they fall asleep. There was no way I could have done the latter because of my own night terrors as a child.

For about seven years, I did not sleep for a full night in the bed beside George. I was sleeping by the kids or the kids were sleeping by me. I usually had more than one mattress to a room. I fearfully shut my eyes, not knowing what the next morning would bring. I still thought I could create some sort of normalcy or safety for us. But then I made everything worse.

CHAPTER TEN

The Scarlet Letter

EARLY IN 2010, I TURNED FORTY, and George threw a big party for me at Cilantro's, a restaurant and bar where we'd gone to whoop it up when we were young. It was a fun night, his way of repaying me for the year of celebration that accompanied his fortieth. George had asked for my help designing the invitation, which used his nickname for me. "Blondie is turning 40," it read: "Come help her." I tried to keep it simple because that's how I'd have celebrated if it were up to me—a quiet night with my family. I have a hard time being the center of attention. George invited a lot of people and most of them showed up, which surprised me. I really appreciated him doing that.

The night was a rare reprieve from George's rages. The rest of the time we were caught in what felt like an endless, terrible loop I couldn't escape. I needed change but didn't know how to effect it. So, I did the most clichéd and damaging thing I could: in 2010, after two years of emotional support from my kid's hockey coach, I began a physical affair with him.

It wasn't driven by romantic interest or even lust on my part. Rather than turning to drugs or alcohol, I used someone else to numb my pain. That's not a justification, just an explanation. I'd counsel anyone in a similar situation to sit down and look closely at her life and relationship. Why are you turning to someone else? What are you avoiding? Will this create lasting damage? I wish I had done that.

The physical part of the affair began in the summer, triggered by spite. The day before, George had raged at me non-stop before getting on a plane; I was hurt. I had been talking to this other man, sharing intimate details of my life with him, for more than two years. I asked myself, "How could a physical relationship be any different?"

There was nothing cinematic about the affair. It was more like high school kids sneaking around to have sex, whether at the arena, a hotel room, or in my car. We got together only a few times before I realized I couldn't live with the guilt, or the fear. I knew I had to end it, which I did in early 2011.

"I can't do this," I told X. "I have to figure out what's going on in my marriage." He said he was worried about me, and kept checking in all the time. It would be everything from "Hey sexy, can we go for lunch?" to "How are the kids doing for tryouts?" I'd delete the messages immediately, sometimes after responding. Of course, I shouldn't have responded at all. I could see I wasn't drawing a clear line with him but, at the same time, I needed his emotional support. As I mentioned earlier, this man had been sexually abused by his father as a child. He explained the dynamics of abuse to me in a way I could understand.

By this time, I was aware that George was monitoring my communications. In the middle of the night, he had downloaded spyware onto my phone. I am a heavy sleeper and only noticed something was wrong when I found that my battery had started draining quickly. George would log onto my phone from his computer and read all my texts. He was logging on and off throughout the day. He had to catch texts in real time if he were to see them at all, because I would immediately delete messages from X.

Late in the summer of 2011, our family went on a trip to China, one of the perfectly choreographed all-out vacations George liked to orchestrate. By then, I had begun to see our annual family trips as a facade. To look at photographs of our travels to Mexico, France, Italy, and China, it would seem that everything was perfect, but I was becoming acutely aware of the contrast between the reality of my life behind closed doors and these trips.

On our return from China, I decided I had to be honest with George about the affair. I didn't feel good about myself and my behaviour, and I felt hypocritical because I was holding George's affairs against him. In fact, I felt like I was becoming him. If I was going to expect truthfulness in our marriage, I had to demonstrate it myself. My hope was that doing so would create the change we needed. That, I would learn, was naive.

I ended up telling George that September day out of necessity, not choice. George had blown up at me the day before. I'd just dropped off skates for X to sharpen because I was avoiding direct contact with him, but he asked me via text if I would swing by and take him to lunch. Still feeling vulnerable after the blow-up, and finding it hard to wean myself from X's advice and support, I agreed.

I turned the car around and picked him up to grab Tim Horton's down the street. George was supposed to be at the Economic Forum in Banff, where Mark Carney was speaking. But, while I was in the car with X, I received a text from George: "Hey, do you want to go for lunch? Where are you?"

I knew immediately he had read my texts. I was overcome with fear. "Get out of the car, now," I told X.

I called George and asked why he wasn't in Banff.

"I stayed to be with you," he said.

"I think we should talk," I said.

I was shaking—disclosing the affair felt like jumping off a cliff—but I knew I couldn't go on the way things were.

I explained to George that I regretted my actions and that I wanted us to go to counselling. "I've been trying to tell you for ages I'm not happy," I said. "I bought all these books and you wouldn't go to therapy with me." I told him that if we couldn't communicate and figure out what was failing between us, we should go our own ways.

George couldn't believe what I'd told him. He was dumbfounded. His immediate response was to plead that he wanted to make the marriage work. He'd see a therapist, do whatever it took. If he couldn't have me, he said, he would kill himself. That night, he decided he needed distance and drove to the mountain house. While there, he went through our wedding album and texted me to say he wanted to kill himself. The night he came back, he slept in the closet in a fetal position.

The days after his return were a blur of anger-fueled texts, calls, and conversations. I was attached to my phone, constantly checking it. We went to the therapist I was seeing and asked how to manage the situation.

"Do you want a divorce?" she asked.

"No," we both replied.

She told us the obvious. If we wanted to stay married, we had work to do. She added that it would be best if we could keep our problems as much as possible from the kids.

One day, George called from work to say he was driving home and that he wanted me to call X and tell him to stay away from me and the children. I knew George was monitoring my calls, so I stopped at a pay phone and called X to warn him the call was coming. His response frightened me. "Okay, I'm going to tell you something and I want you to listen," X said. "He's going to go after you and you're not going to be safe and it's going to be the worst it ever has been. You have to know that you can call the police."

Until then, I never considered calling the police. I thanked him for his support and said goodbye.

I went home and called X as instructed. George was there to tape the conversation. Afterwards, he would send parts of it to me and to the children as one of his tactics of torment.

The affair gave George license, in his mind, to do whatever he wanted. He felt he had the moral high ground. He was also worried that his control over me was lessening, so he tried to control how other people saw me. A couple of days after my admission, George came home from work and he'd been drinking. He poured himself a tumbler of Scotch and invited friends from the neighbourhood over. Then he announced to them that I had fucked around with a hockey coach, a black guy who was toothless, as if those details made it worse. (Like many hockey players, X had lost teeth and wore dentures.)

George reported back to me on what people he had told about my affair were saying, things like "That's intolerable," and "She shouldn't get away with it!" Others came up to me personally, knowing George's own habits: "It's about fucking time," one said. George's extramarital dalliances were well-known, but I didn't stop to think about the double standard.

Before long, I was the pariah of the neighbourhood. The wives of George's friends and most of my friends sided with George: most of them felt my actions were wrong. It was as if I was the first person in Calgary to have an extramarital affair. I felt like Hester Prynne in *The Scarlet Letter*.

George also called my mother and father to tell them about the affair, but my parents didn't want to hear about it. They wrestled with what they sensed was going on in our marriage but they had never asked about it. My father was aware of George's anger, of his punching holes in the wall. More than once, he advised me to get a restraining order but I knew that would only make matters worse. There was also willful blindness on my parents' part: they knew George drank a lot but they wanted me to have what looked, from the outside, like a perfect marriage. They appreciated from afar how the kids appeared to be thriving. They did offer me support after George's call, as did some friends, but it wasn't enough to protect me from the uncontrollable, manic anger the affair provoked in George.

CHAPTER ELEVEN

Fear and Torment

AFTER GEORGE LEARNED ABOUT my affair, my home—the place we're supposed to be the safest—became the most dangerous place for me to be. I tried to restore an equilibrium. I tried desperately to do everything to George's exacting standards. It didn't prevent me from being berated: I was now a "cunt." George would call or text me while drunk, threatening to hire someone to take X out. Then he would apologize and tell me I should have a friend over or go out with a friend. When I did, he'd rage at me for not being there to support him. It was incredibly destabilizing.

"You will never forgive me, so we might as well just call it off," I'd say.

"I can't live without you," he'd counter.

I still didn't think I was in a violent, abusive marriage. X had opened my eyes to the nature of abuse, but I didn't see myself as someone like Nicole Brown Simpson. I wasn't bruised. Yet.

The physical violence ramped up not long after the affair. Once, I woke up in bed with George's hands around my neck. Twice, at night, I woke to see George standing over me holding onto his penis. In a terrified, disoriented state, I'd ask him what he was doing. "I'm going to urinate on you, you piece of shit," he'd tell me. Other times, I'd wake to see him staring at me, which was equally terrifying.

I'd find ways to explain it away. It's his drinking, I'd think, or I'd blame myself for having had the affair. It still seemed possible to me that, if he could just stabilize his behaviour, he could heal.

I'm sure some people reading are shaking their heads as they read this, and are asking themselves why I would stay in that situation when I had family and access to resources.

The more complicated truth is that I was not sure what to do. I was constantly running calculations in my head. George was abusive and controlling, but he could be giving and supportive. He was all the things people saw: witty, creative, and smart, with a brilliant mind. He was a good father when he wasn't messed up. I asked myself how much I was to blame for his present disposition.

I was doing the same sort of calculations over the kids. I wondered if they were better off with an imperfect father than no father at all. I adhered to the stigma of the "broken home," a phase that suggests homes are broken when parents split, not when they're still together. I knew I didn't want the kids dragged onto the battlefield of our marriage, or used as pawns in George's bids to retaliate against me.

I tried to envision us leaving George, but I had a hard time seeing how I could manage without him. I had no resources, no access to money. I considered myself weak and unworthy, and doubted anyone else could care about me. Most of the time, the question in my mind was not whether or not to leave, but simply how to keep safe. I also worried that, if I did leave, it might be the end of George, since he was constantly threatening suicide.

One night in late September, George came to me in a fury once again about the affair. "How could you have done that to me?" he said, demanding sex. He was getting aggressive. As always, my instinct was to try to keep quiet to protect the kids.

"Let's go into the bathroom," I said.

"You need to make me feel better," he kept saying.

Before I knew what was happening, he had shoved me down onto the granite steps leading to the bathtub. Then he was on top of me, choking me.

This is more force than I've experienced, I thought.

I struggled against him while worrying where Isla was. Could she hear us? I fought to extract myself, telling George I thought I heard one of the kids downstairs and had to find out what was going on. He agreed. As I got up, I glanced over at my phone on the counter. George knew I was frightened enough to call 911. He grabbed my phone. "Go find out what that noise is," he ordered.

I went downstairs and used the landline to call the police. George followed me and heard me hang up. We looked at each other helplessly. He called me a "fucking cunt" and went to find Carter and Isla, who were huddled together in her room. John was at hockey camp. "Your mom called the cops on me, and I'm going to jail," he told them.

George began freaking out even more, raving about how he'd never be given an Order of Canada now. He had received countless awards over the years—several from the University of Calgary; the Queen Elizabeth II Silver Jubilee medal from the premier of Alberta; the honour of being named one of 200 Young Global Leaders by the World Economic Forum—but the Order of Canada was the one he coveted. Being found out as a domestic abuser would ruin his chances. That's what he was most concerned about.

As we waited for the police, I suddenly realized I needed to change clothes. I had unknowingly urinated on myself when George began choking me.

Two male cops showed up. They separated us, which is standard. Cops don't like "domestics," the single greatest category of police calls in most cities. They're volatile and dangerous. George explained that he was extremely upset about my affair. He managed to charm his cop and gain his sympathy. "I lost control," he said. The cop began confiding first to George, then to me, about his own marriage. He and his wife had divorced and he regretted it.

The officer I spoke to lectured me. "You have kids," he said. "Your husband is hurt and you have to understand men have egos." There were marks on my neck, the beginning of bruises, but he didn't ask about them.

The officers told us we should work on our marriage. Both agreed they would be upset if they found out their wife had screwed around.

George left to spend the night at Le Germain, a hotel-apartment complex across from his office. A police report was filed, but no charges were laid. It didn't cross my mind to lay charges. Nor did I think of it as attempted rape. It would take #MeToo for me to put it in that context.

Two days later, a social worker came to the kids' school to speak to them. Isla was then in grade five, Carter in grade nine, and John in grade twelve. The social worker asked a series of questions: "Are you in fear of your dad? Does your dad beat your mom?" Whatever the kids said, they managed to allay his concerns. They knew how to cover. When they got home, they were clearly upset. Being pulled out of class had embarrassed them.

A social worker was also sent to George's office. He recommended counselling for George as well as for the children, although there was no follow-up. George was mortified about the visit. He came home and continued to rage. Again, it was all my fault. That night was one of the nights when I woke up with him standing over me, ready to urinate.

After George had spent the night at Le Germain that one time, we both agreed it wasn't smart for him to drink—if he drank, he should just go to a hotel. It became okay for him to have that space.

Life went on. We continued to present and travel like a happy couple. The annual shooting trip to England was scheduled for October and, despite everything, he wanted me to accompany him. After the assault in the bathroom, I told him that I wouldn't travel with him because he was violent. But he would not relent, saying he wanted me with him and that he deserved it after what I had done. I made him sign a contract, written by our therapist, saying he wouldn't hurt me.

We went to London for a couple of days before the shoot. George was on antidepressants and ADD medication at the time, and wasn't supposed to drink. We went to a sous vide restaurant, where he sat down and said "I'm not going to eat here and not drink." The more he drank, the most hostile he became. The atmosphere of the meal was tense, and I prayed for any outside distraction—the waiter, a loud group beside us, anything—to relieve the stress of one another's company. We got through it.

During the shoot, however, George was well-behaved. Our group stayed at the same inn as usual, where the rooms are small. He knew any angry behaviour would be exposed.

The following month, in November, George and I traveled to Washington with Carter's hockey team. Thanks to George's political contacts, the team visited the Canadian embassy. I have a photo from the trip that shows Carter, George, and me on its splendid patio, with the Capitol Building in the background. Carter stands in between us in a hockey jacket and we're all smiling, but I look hollowed-out. There's no light behind my eyes.

The other parents traveled on the bus with the team, but George insisted we have our own car. As everyone else took a city tour, George and I explored a little art colony. He stopped as we walked by a tattoo parlor.

"If you loved me, you would get my name tattooed on your body," he said. "That would mean something to me."

"Where?" I asked him, uninterested.

"On your boob," he told me.

This was part of the sexual territoriality my affair had unleashed in George. Before the affair, he suggested I have nude photos done by a professional photographer: "You're so beautiful, but you're gonna lose it, so you better get it done," he'd say. I objected. After the affair, he pressed the issue again: I had betrayed him, he argued, so I owed him nude photos. It was a penance, or extortion. Anyway, I agreed, and afterwards he would send me texts of the photos when he knew I was in public to embarrass and humiliate me. Often this happened when I was sitting in close quarters at a kids' hockey game.

As we drove around Washington in the sedan, George was forlorn. He began flipping through pictures of us on his phone, and told me how much he wished our marriage was like that of another couple we knew, one of George's associates and his wife. Almost on cue, his phone buzzed with a text: it was from the very friend whose marriage he wanted us to emulate. I looked at the screen, and all I could see was a pair of massive, naked female breasts. They belonged to the woman his friend was having an affair with, the wife of another one of George's business partners. As I said, a small world.

"Yeah, it would be great to have a marriage like their marriage," I said, laughing at the absurdity of it all.

Meanwhile my sister had moved back to Calgary. She had gone overseas with her family in 2007, returning in 2010. Now she had heard a rumor that George was having an affair with an old girlfriend, a woman he'd split up with before we got together, although they kept in touch and he sometimes referred to her as "the love of my life." Kathy was told that they would get together when George was shooting in Spain; he'd break off from the group and visit her.

Kathy took it upon herself to write a letter to this woman, hoping it would help me break free from the fear and torment. "If you knew about it, you would be able to do something," she said. I didn't want her to send the letter, but I knew I couldn't control what Kathy did. She kept telling me that everybody was talking about how George screwed around.

After Kathy contacted the woman, she, in turn, forwarded the message to George while he and I were in British Columbia watching John play junior hockey. "What the fuck, Karen?" he said to me, forcing me to read it, and looked at me with a piercing hatred that my children still talk about. Afterward, I told Kathy that I appreciated her concern, but that all I got from it was a weekend of torment.

In the meantime, we had returned to therapy. George would arrive at appointments with more pages ripped from my journal. The therapist I had begun seeing in 2008 nursed us through the first stages of George finding out about my affair, and I also began seeing another therapist whom I liked, partly because she promised a magical solution. "You're easy," she said. "I'm going to work with you for three months and your world is going to change." She suggested I bring in George, and she'd work on the both of us. George came to a few sessions, and decided he wanted her as his therapist. That therapist started seeing him, too, which is against the rules, and simply led to her being caught in the crossfire between us: a completely unhealthy situation. Finally, it was determined she would see George and I'd find someone else.

My next therapist reminded me of Linda Richman, the *Saturday Night Live* "Coffee Talk" character played by Martin Short. She'd chew gum during sessions and her office was a mess, but she did offer good advice.

All of our therapists said that if we wanted to stay together—and we both agreed we did want to stay together—we had to work to do. There are reasons why affairs occur, like needs not being met, and we had to work on them. In the meantime, we would keep everything under wraps. "Don't tell anyone," we were advised. "Keep it under cover. It's damaging for kids, it's damaging for you to talk about it. You have to move on."

But we didn't move on.

CHAPTER TWELVE

The Beginning
of the End

I N 2012, I BECAME THE VERSION OF my mother who sat on the stairs immobilized by emotions, except that I was usually locked in the bathroom with George raging outside, my head clasped in my hands, my mind oscillating between fearing for my life and feeling sorry for myself. Before the affair, I had figured out how to function and make him the center of the universe, and do everything I could to make him happy. I would wake up in the morning and wonder what I could do to satisfy George and avoid conflict. After the affair, I would wake up knowing that conflict was inevitable, and think about how to minimize it.

I used my journal as a personal cheerleader, writing on New Year's Day: "This is going to be a good year! I know it, I feel it!" Several pages later, the optimism sputtered out into self-rebuke, with a page of "I am using this relationship like a crutch, it is time to let it go" written over and over, like a mantra.

George's threats of suicide increased. He had stopped taking medications, as he usually did when he started to feel better. He felt he no longer needed the pills, and he was uncomfortable with the common side effect of erectile disfunction. Being on and off meds in this way made him still more volatile.

He agreed to see a psychiatrist that February, but wanted it to be at the Scripps Clinic in California so no one in Calgary would find out. The doctor at Scripps diagnosed George with a bipolar disorder, and put him on a long list of medications. They didn't help. If anything, he seemed worse.

The bipolar diagnosis was one of many he'd had after first being told he had ADD in the 1990s. Various doctors had prescribed various pills, which George augmented with steroids and alcohol. If he didn't like one doctor, he'd go to another. There was no consistency in how he was treated, and no follow-up appointments.

After Scripps, we went to the much-hyped Amen Clinic in Costa Mesa, California, which caters to a wealthy population concerned about mental health and willing to pay anything to improve it. We both got PET scans of our brains, and a medical exam in which we were told our health risks. It cost a small fortune, and we learned nothing of value. He continued to be volatile after our trips.

When I say George was more volatile, I mean that his attacks on me by 2012 were relentless. He'd tell me that without him I was nothing. He still held the affair over my head, constantly threatening to "tell the truth" about me. He would text me, and many of his messages were incoherent, indicating he had been drinking: "Your addition men will be told. I do not want my children being raised by a fucking two-faced host." Sometimes the message was simply "FUCK YOU" in caps. Followed by "You are FUCKING useless. wish I had never met you."

I believed I had it coming and apologized to him repeatedly. "I know I'm useless," I responded to one of his text rants in March, and begged him to quit it. "I don't need to hear it again and again. I'm turning off my phone. I need to have this stop."

Although George threatened me with divorce constantly, my therapist and parents were still optimistic that we could rebuild the marriage. That same month, my father emailed George to offer support. He knew George was taking medications for depression and ADD, and said he'd be happy to answer any questions about them, while warning him that suicidal ideation could be one side effect. My father also expressed sadness over the conflict between us, noting that we'd both made "serious relationship mistakes," and advised us to salvage the relationship for ourselves and the children. "Blaming each other at this stage only perpetuates those stresses," he wrote.

He promised that he and my mother would be there for us as we worked to build a new relationship.

My father also said that he hoped George could transfer his success in the business world to rebuilding the family: "If you can develop new businesses then you have the ability to build a new relationship with your family and wife," my dad wrote. "You have to be positive and proactive."

That wasn't happening. My calling the police had intensified George's anger and his need for control, which translated into increased financial control and technological surveillance over me.

Financial control in damaged relationships takes many forms: keeping the abused partner on a restrictive allowance, punishing overspending, ruining their credit rating by maxing out credit cards, hiding joint funds. I once met a woman married to a man worth some $500 million who was denied any access to joint funds, and was forced to rely on a separate "trust fund" he had set up for her. Because the amount varied from year to year, she could never plan. It was a way of keeping her on a leash.

Another couple I know once had money and lost it in a downturn. They have an "open relationship": he can have sex with other women, but she cannot have relationships with other men. She wants out but she's scared to death of her husband, and who strings her along by saying there is serious money coming her way. In order to complete his "big deal," however, he needs to be married and look like a credible family man, the type someone would want to do business with. When the deal is done, he tells her, they will divide the assets and go their separate ways. She lives on a shoestring budget, looking after the children, while he travels the world with his girlfriends, spending money on them.

Another woman who, like me, did not have access to the family financials decided to do something about it. Her husband worked at home in a locked office. One day, when he was drunk and had passed out, she got a key cut and soon after learned what she wanted to learn about the financials while he was out of the house. Her husband had so misrepresented their affairs to her—he had far more money than he'd admitted—that she went straight to a divorce lawyer. The point is that an affluent woman can be mega-rich on paper but functionally poor. She can drive an $80,000 car registered in her husband's name and carry an expensive bag, yet have no access to family bank accounts and not enough cash to survive a week on her own.

George would tell me that he was sharing every financial success and failure with me, but in fact I was kept in the dark about the family's financial life throughout the marriage. Whenever George needed my signature, he'd put only the signature page in front of me and ask me to sign. I didn't ask questions, even when my sixth sense told me that he was having problems, or I'd have to listen to him belittle my abilities. If I caught him on an inconsistency, he'd turn it around and say, "How many times do I have to go over this stuff with you? You don't listen; it goes in one ear and out the other."

When he was really vicious, he would accuse me of having early-onset dementia and suggest I go see my father or my brother, both of whom are neurologists. During our arguments, I would sometimes excuse myself and go to the washroom to write on my phone what he was telling me: I honestly didn't know if the problem was my inability to retain information or if he was feeding me inconsistent numbers.

For the most part, I chose not to engage him on the question of finances. There was enough tension at home, and I had to pick my battles carefully: fighting with him about money was usually a losing proposition for me. He was masterful with numbers, and he'd turn the conversation around to make me out as an ingrate for the gifts and comfort he provided our family. "Do I not look after you and the kids?" he'd ask. "Take that necklace and tennis bracelet and throw it in the river. I am a fucking idiot . . . You are dragging me down. Five suicide attempts."

After the affair, any financial request I had, whether for airline tickets for me and the kids, school tuitions, or other big purchases, had to be approved by George or George's assistant. The latter had more access to our financial transactions—bank accounts, all bills, tax information—than I did. George told me he'd changed the bank accounts, and that I was allowed to use only a Visa and a debit card.

He would bully me about money, telling me that, if we divorced, I'd have to go on *Auto Trader* to look for an '86 Rabbit. A couple of times, George cut up my credit cards in the middle of the night. Once when I was leaving to host a lunch for the Calgary Philharmonic, he said, "Have a good lunch," in a tone that made me suspicious. Sure enough, when I went to pay, none of my cards were accepted. I'd taken out cash as a backup, suspecting he might do that to me, so I managed to avoid the embarrassment he had wanted me to experience.

When I told my then-therapist (the one who was seeing us both separately) about George putting financial pressure on me and my inability to deal with him, she tried to bolster my confidence: "You are not a loser," she wrote in an email. "His pride is very hurt, and divorce seems like the only answer to him. I will see him later and hopefully slow down the train." The train never slowed.

He also stepped up his surveillance of me. I knew that any time I went online, my texts and emails would be monitored by George or his assistant. After the affair, I just accepted the fact he would be reading everything. I'd tell myself I deserved it, and that I had nothing to hide.

Once, George blew a gasket after the father of a girl in Isla's dance class texted me to ask if I liked a particular band. "What did you do to egg this on?" he demanded. Another evening, as I was waiting for Isla to finish ballet class alongside other parents, he called to yell at me that I was a whore. I got up and walked out of the room with the phone pressed tightly to my ear, furiously pushing down the volume so people could not hear his profanity. He started to read back a text of mine from someone who told me they'd enjoyed our evening and that they loved me very much. The text sounded familiar, and I interrupted to ask for the phone number associated with the text. It was my dad's number—we'd had dinner together two nights previously. George hung up. When I returned home, not a word was mentioned. It was like it didn't happen.

Yet another day, I tried to log onto my Shaw webmail account and found that my password had been changed. I couldn't change it back or access my account. Only the person on the billing account could do that: in other words, George's assistant. I went into a Shaw store and convinced the person to help me change my password by claiming that my husband was out of the country.

His behaviour was taking a toll on me. I saw, sometimes starkly, the peril my marriage posed to me and the kids. "Leave or die," I wrote in my journal. But I felt alone, and that terrified me. I believed no one cared, and I doubted I could survive on my own. I was worried everything I had would evaporate: my children, the few people that remained supportive from "our" friends, the pleasure I derived from being involved in the community. George would tell me that it was all because of him that I was invited to sit on the board of the Calgary Philharmonic Orchestra. "I fucking called them and bought your position," he texted. "There you go you useless POS. I never wanted to tell you that but I wanted you to believe in yourself. Now I don't."

I was also growing more frustrated with the tenor of my life and its value system, its privilege, and its focus on material possessions. I'd remind myself that if I had nothing, I would be okay. I knew I could get a job at the department store where I worked when I was sixteen. I would have no trouble getting by with a simpler lifestyle, and neither would the kids. We were perfectly happy buying things on sale at Winners and Nordstrom Rack. George was the one obsessed with brand names and material things.

But I couldn't decide to leave. I vacillated between "I don't deserve his bullying" and "I'm a bad person who shouldn't have done this to the family." I was filled with remorse about the affair. "Why did I do that?" I asked in the journal. "Was my life really that bad?"

My frustration with my predicament and my indecision got expressed in reckless behaviour. I was super-aggressive while driving. On one occasion, I lashed out at a woman who complained I didn't have my dogs on leash in the dog park. I knew she had a valid point, but that didn't stop me from losing it. I asked her what made her think she had any right to tell me what to do, told her to mind her own fucking business, and capped it off by mocking what she was wearing. Thinking of it now makes me want to curl up into a ball of shame.

One night that spring, George decided to sleep in a hotel rather than come home. He phoned me the next day to say he'd overdosed the previous night on sleeping pills. "I can't take my head off the pillow," he said. "You made me do this." I went to the hotel to check on him while Isla waited for me to take her to a Kiwanis festival to compete in a series of musical theatre numbers she had been rehearsing all year long. She had solos, duets, and group numbers. George knew it was a big day for her, and that many people were relying on her, but it didn't matter to him. He told me he had a headache and was super-sensitive to light, but he was adamant that I didn't call an ambulance. "You'll ruin my career," he told me. "No one would trust me."

Even when he was out of the house, George was a constant presence in my days. He was in touch, relentlessly, by text. To this day, hearing a phone ping is triggering for me. He would text me, repeatedly threatening suicide, then tell me he hadn't been a good husband, that he'd been abusive and drank too much. "I failed at that and will have to take that to my deathbed. I'm ready to go now Karen, it's time." And then . . . radio silence. The silences could produce as much anxiety in me as the texts.

Before long, however, he'd be texting me again but with the tables turned: "You have wrecked my life and I can legitimately claim that know [sic] Thank you Karen. You have killed the good person inside of me."

Serial texting was always a signal that George was drinking. On a trip I had taken to Los Angeles, where Isla was dancing competitively, I was up all night dealing with a barrage of texts.

"I have to go to bed," I'd plead.

"You can't leave me now," he'd say. "I'm going to do something you will regret."

So why not turn off my phone? Honestly, I couldn't. I was the only functioning adult and needed to be available for the children. I also couldn't live with the thought that I might kill George if I failed to answer a call. So I would wait for George's texts and calls, as distressing as they were. But, amid all the insults, there would be short bursts where George would tell me how much he loved me, and that for me was part of the problem. I would cling to these moments. In one, he told me how much he missed me, and how he wanted me to go to London with him, sounding like the positive, affectionate person I wanted to believe I had married. He would say that he wanted us to be together, and promise to show me the financials.

It was because of one of those moments that I agreed to travel with him in May, a decision I will always regret.

CHAPTER THIRTEEN

Argentina

I N MAY OF 2012, GEORGE AND I TRAVELED to South America for a week—first to Santiago, Chile, then to Buenos Aires, Argentina. George had board work and thought it would be good for us to get away. I'd always wanted to go to Argentina and that, along with his momentary sweetness, was enough to get me to agree to accompany him, although I was still nervous. We traveled with the joint understanding that neither of us would drink.

With George working in Santiago, I spent the day exploring on my own. I visited art museums. I hiked to the top of Cerro San Cristóbal to see the statue of the Virgin Mary. I sat in the cathedral for most of that afternoon, drawn to the quiet, protected space. When I think back to that afternoon now, I wonder if I sensed that I needed it. Was I beginning to understand the significance of religion for people in dire need? I prayed, asking my higher power to guide me and to soften George's heart. On my way out, I took two wallet-size pamphlets of the Virgin Mary with a prayer on the back. I wanted to keep that protection and comfort with me. I still keep one on my nightstand.

In Buenos Aires, we spent a day binge shopping as a relationship anesthetic. That was typically how George and I spent time when traveling: we'd hit our dopamine buttons by buying, taking things back to the hotel, removing items from bags, putting them on. In Argentina, we bought bone-handled knives that were never used and leather jackets we never wore.

Two nights before we left, George took a photograph of me on the hotel's sweeping staircase as we were leaving for dinner. I look wary, and I'm wearing a dress I'd bought that afternoon. I'd never wear it again. I gave it away; I didn't want anything to remind me of what happened next.

First, however, we went to a great restaurant. "I'm not going to enjoy this without wine," George told me. I thought about reminding him of our promise but I knew the moment he suggested drinking that I would lose either way. If I spoke up, I'd ruin the evening, and there would be hell to pay for the rest of the vacation. If I went along, there was just a chance we could get through it without trouble. We were getting along okay, and I felt I could use a drink as well.

George loved the ritual of wine. He loved perusing the list, ordering a pricey bottle, then having the staff take him a little more seriously. He was never open to suggestions from the sommelier; he believed he knew more. He'd then do the tasting, the swirling, the sniffing, the first sip.

He ended up ordering two bottles. I had two glasses; he drank the rest. Everything seemed okay at the time, but I was monitoring the situation as always. I didn't see any red flags at first. But then, something shifted. As the alcohol took effect, George become more difficult and I swung into high alert.

After dinner, George wanted to go to the hotel bar for an after-dinner drink, which was something we often did when we traveled. He'd order a Scotch and I'd never know what to order because I never wanted a drink late in the evening. We'd usually observe the people around us and talk about our day but, this night, there wasn't much to talk about. It was winter, and off-season, so the bar was both cold and empty. Everything was dead.

Returning to the hotel, I tried not to trigger him in any way. When we got to the room, George headed to bed, and seemed to fall asleep, which was a relief. When I went to join him, he was lying on his stomach, sprawled on the diagonal. As softly as I could, I asked him to move over. Suddenly, he flipped over and sprang, as if he'd been waiting.

He began to throw things. First a mirror shattered, then the glass on a large framed picture. After he finished trashing the room, he turned to me. He wanted sex, he said, pushing me down on the floor. Suddenly, he was on top of me, his knees on my shoulders and legs pinning down my arms. I couldn't move. I felt his hands around my neck choking me. Then I felt his closed fist on my face and shoulders, punching me again and again. I saw stars, and heard bells, like the ones you see on Looney Tunes. The more I fought back, the harder he hit, so I stop fighting. I felt like I was having an out-of-body experience. I was hovering on the ceiling, watching a man beat the hell out of his wife.

As quickly as George jumped on me, he stopped, as if he'd come out of a trance. I watched him walk into the bathroom. Before I knew it, he was back by my side on the floor, and telling me he'd swallowed all of his sleeping pills. "Take my hand," he instructed.

I was confused and disoriented.

"What are you talking about?" I asked.

"I'm going to die now," George said. "I can't live with myself for what I've done. Hold my hand."

My mind scrambled. What should I do? Call 911, or whatever 911 is in Argentina? Call the front desk? Call the Canadian Embassy? George had announced he was overdosing on sleeping pills many times before; I knew he had to take a lot and that whatever he'd taken would make him drowsy, and then he would sleep.

I waited until he was drowsy, and then turned him on his side and stuck my fingers down his throat. Eventually, I got him to throw up most of the pills on the carpet. Later when I told a friend what had happened, leaving out the brutal assault, he asked how I knew how to do that. "Years of living with bulimia came in handy," I told him. That friend and I share a morbid sense of humour.

The next day was all gloom, cloudy, and rainy. George and I left the room to walk around. I put on sunglasses, and looked for a pharmacy where I could buy makeup to cover the bruising on my face. George helped me pick out the right color of purple eye shadow to balance with the darkness around my eye.

We were unusually silent. We walked through La Recoleta Cemetery, where Evita Perón is buried. It is filled with elaborately carved scroll-work and pillars that only reach as high as your shoulders. All the structures are weirdly small; it's more magical than macabre. George walked with his head hung in shame.

It started to pour rain as we returned to the hotel. We were walking on a slanted sidewalk and my ballet flats didn't have any treads, so I kept slipping. Pretty soon, George was doing the same. Neither of us were able to stand on solid ground, so we clung to each other. That was our marriage in a nutshell.

We were soaked and exhausted by the time we returned to our room. It was as if the night before had never happened. The shattered glass was gone, the carpet looked like new. Anything can be fixed for enough money, I thought. They probably deal with similar scenes all the time.

That night, we went out for dinner with an Argentinian colleague of George's. Again, the scene was surreal. I wore sunglasses to hide the increasingly visible bruises on my face. If this colleague of George's thought the sunglasses were odd, he didn't indicate it.

The following day, travelling home, George and I sat across from one another in business class. He apologized for beating me. "I'm going to fix it," he said. "I'm going to quit drinking."

Then he told me that I needed to commit to therapy. Then he said he needed a drink. Then, he said he deserved a drink because of everything I had done to him. As the alcohol kicked in, he went into "It's all your fault" mode. He told me people were laughing at what I had done, referring to my affair. "Your name is shit downtown," he said.

George stared me down until he fell into a drunken sleep. The next day, back at home in Calgary, he asked why I stayed with him. "I love you and I believe you can do this," I told him. I truly wanted to believe it was the alcohol that made him mean and that, if he wasn't drinking, he'd be a different person.

Also after we got home, I did something for myself: I took a selfie to document the assault. It's still on my phone. In the photo, my eye is ringed red, purple and brown. There's a big bruise on the side of my nose. The severity of that violent attack was a wake-up call. I couldn't pretend I wasn't in Nicole Brown Simpson territory anymore. It occurred to me that George was treating me like he treated our dogs. He'd pet them, show them affection, and then twist their ears until they yelped.

I knew I had to end it. I just didn't know how to end it—or how complicated that would be. After interviewing a few lawyers, I found one that I liked. Laurie Allen was a strong, no bullshit woman whose voice sounded like she smoked a pack of Player's a day. She was someone you didn't fuck with, and someone who wouldn't be intimidated by George.

I made an appointment with her, and scheduled it at the same day and time as George and I had a therapy appointment. When I didn't show up, George began texting and calling. "Where are you?" he asked. "Seeing a lawyer," I answered.

His response was succinct: "Fuck you!"

In the lawyer's office, I put George on speakerphone. He told me he wouldn't let me in the house and that I'd never see the kids, and threatened to put my things on the driveway. Laurie interrupted in her no-nonsense, don't-fuck-with-me tone. "George, you are being unreasonable," she said. She told him she could get a court order to make him leave the house that afternoon. She was measured but firm: "Karen is the primary caregiver. She's not leaving the residence."

She told George she'd prefer to speak with his lawyer; he gave her the name of the lawyer he had used when his first engagement ended. "Perfect, I know her," Laurie said. "I'll contact her." She then suggested George leave the house for the weekend and be co-operative for the sake of the children.

When the conversation ended, Laurie asked if I wanted her to file a restraining order. I didn't, intuitively knowing that a restraining order would only escalate the abuse. She gave me her cell number, telling me she never did that for clients. "Call me if you're in danger," she said.

It was evident she saw risk. "I'm sorry, but he hit you," she said. "You have to draw the line somewhere. Personally, I would never let a man put a finger on me."

I remember thinking, "But he just hit me that one time. He doesn't do it all the time. And no kidding, no one would raise a finger to her. I'm not her."

Hours later, George left a series of texts threatening self-harm, and didn't say where he was going. I heard nothing more for hours, which was unusual. As night got nearer, I began to panic. Had he actually killed himself?

When I didn't hear anything that night, I called the RCMP close to our mountain house to check the property. Finally, I located George, who'd stayed the night at a hotel. He told me he'd taken a bunch of pills, but he was fine.

We had a calm conversation. He was apologetic, but said consulting a lawyer was a betrayal. He said he wanted to work on us and that he wanted to live. He talked about fearing the consequences if I left him, what it would look like, how horrible his life would be. He promised to stop drinking and control his anger. My body was begging me to be convinced. I allowed myself to be convinced.

After not being able to track down George, his assistant and I agreed that we would communicate if either of us heard from George when he went missing. She agreed to openly communicate to me on this matter and would not wait to receive his approval.

Laurie gave me the weekend to think about starting divorce proceedings, and I spent the time oscillating from wanting a divorce to wanting to be with George, and wishing everything would just calm down. My parents knew I'd gone to a lawyer, and that there was conflict in the marriage, although I never told them details. My father mentioned getting a restraining order again and again, to the point I stopped talking about what was going on. What people don't know is that restraining orders don't always help women in abusive situations; sometimes they incite anger on the part of the person named in the order, which can put women at more risk.

I had found a temporary escape and some new direction in late May at the five-day Hoffman Process retreat outside of Calgary. The program, founded by Bob Hoffman in 1967, is a global affair known for famous attendees such as Justin Bieber. The purpose is to help people identify negative behaviours, moods, and ways of thinking that develop unconsciously and are conditioned in childhood. One focus is parental issues: everything boils down to attachment. While I was at Hoffman, I realized that, by marrying someone who had problems with addiction and mental illness, I was recreating childhood dynamics. It opened my eyes to my relations with my parents and my constant need for my father's approval. It also made me realize that I always placed my own needs far behind everyone else's. I never asked myself what I wanted, or what I felt.

One condition of the retreat is that you write a letter to someone. Of course, I wrote to George. I poured out my heart. He thought it was naked and awful—and then berated me for not writing him daily. George had feared the program would change my life and that I'd move out. Rather, at the end of it, I felt recharged enough to go home.

The tranquility didn't last. The day I left Hoffman was a beautiful spring day, and I thought I'd surprise Isla by picking her up at her rehearsal at Young Canadians, a music and dance program for talented kids from all socioeconomic levels subsidized by the Stampede Foundation. The kids were working towards performing at the Stampede grandstand show. I had missed Isla, and wanted to express my love and gratitude to her. All of the talk of parent-child bonding at the retreat made me want to reaffirm my commitment to being a better female role model for her.

As I waited with the other parents, I received a call from George. I answered to hear him screaming at the top of his lungs that I was a whore, a cunt. He was yelling so loudly, there was no doubt that the other parents could hear him. I was pressing the phone against my ear so hard it hurt while madly turning the volume down and walking towards the car.

I had ruined life for him, George told me. He was the laughing stock of Calgary, and I would pay for what I did. As he was yelling, I saw Isla looking lost, as if she thought no one was there for her. She was eleven. I told George I had to go, but he called about ten times between me picking up Isla and getting back into the car. My heart was racing and I was freezing on a warm spring day. Isla could tell something was wrong. "Are you okay, Mommy?" she asked. I realized I had forgotten to tell her I loved her and wanted to be a role model for her. Now there was no point.

George kept calling. I asked Isla to hang on: "I just need to get this call from Dad." I finally answered and he said, "Karen, why haven't you been answering the phone? I was phoning to tell you I love you and I am so sorry. I am threatened. I think I should go to Hoffman, too."

I wanted to laugh but instead said, "Thanks George, I appreciate you saying you are sorry. Yes, you should definitely consider Hoffman."

And at that moment my body was better, my mind was better. It was that same, almost biological need for tension and release. I was then able to have a much better connection with my little girl, and to try and be that female mentor.

George's pledge to make things better was short-lived. At the end of May, he came into the dining room where John and Carter were studying for finals. He played them the recording of conversation he'd made of me calling X to tell him that I didn't want anything to do with him. "Your mother is a whore," he told them. "You see what a fuck-up she is? She has ruined the family, and you, too."

I watched the scene unfold from the doorway with growing fear. "You don't need to do this with the kids," I told George. "This is between me and you."

As George played the recording, John stood up and responded to his father with a fury I'd never seen from him. He picked up a dining room chair and threw it at the wall, as he'd seen George do many times. "Stop fucking tormenting us and her," he said.

While this was going on, I texted my sister, who arrived to take the kids. I had learned having a third party present tended to diffuse George's anger. It was his hyper-consciousness of how things appeared to others.

"Are you okay?" Kathy asked when she showed up.

"Yes," I told her, feeling a surge of gratitude.

I had missed having Kathy and the rest of my family in my life. I was realizing how important they were, and I had been becoming more vocal with George, and in front of the children, about wanting my family back in my life. Kathy's presence that evening convinced George to storm off to bed, defusing a difficult situation.

Around this same time, my family helped me in another way: by insisting we get George's guns out of the house. It's a well-established fact that the mere presence of guns in a household substantially increases the risk of violence. George owned several guns and kept them under lock, including his matched pair of handmade Boss & Co. 12-bore side-by-side shotguns. He also owned a Benelli Super Black Eagle 12-gauge waterfowl gun that he kept in a gun locker at home, and a 410-gauge used for smaller birds, gophers, and squirrels. After George began threatening suicide, I asked the man who did our home maintenance to take them away, locker and all. Everyone, including my parents, his parents, and me, wanted the guns out of the house.

George went to Hoffman for five days in June, but the one he went to was in the Sonoma Valley, which is far more luxe than the Canadian version. As I was driving him to the airport he panicked and we started to argue, again on the same theme, something small that escalated into him calling me a whore and a slut. Even as he was calling me names, I could see he was terrified. Part of me wanted to pull up at the airport, kick him out of the car with his bag, and drive away as fast as I could, but I decided I'd try to send him off positively instead, holding his hand to the gate.

I parked the car. He had settled down and we had made it to outside the gate, about to part in a loving way. Just then a good-looking, middle-aged man walked toward us, checking me out, smiling at me. That was it for George. I was back to being a whore again, and he wasn't going to Hoffman. I tried to talk him down, but rational thought was going nowhere.

Finally, I told him that if he didn't go, he wasn't coming home. I would ask for a separation. He marched to the gate, yelling "Fuck off!" at me as he went through to customs.

While he was at Hoffman, he'd send photos of himself meditating, saying he was trying. As always, the messaging was volatile. One minute he'd be telling me he loved me and couldn't live without me; the next, he'd say that he hated me and that I'd ruined his life. But he returned home somewhat changed, a bit softened. "We can change, we can work on it," he said, and he seemed to be trying. He had written me a letter talking about wanting "a new beginning."

There were improvements, but his ranting at me continued. I found myself starting to detach when he'd start up, and start thinking about a grocery list. If I was listening to him on the phone, I could literally put it down and clean the kitchen and, after a few minutes, grab it and say, "Uh huh, yes, you are right."

My therapist was telling me that I needed a year away from him. She told me she thought I had "Stockholm syndrome"—which is not a real thing, but I knew what she meant. I thought she was being harsh.

"He drinks," I said, excusing George's behaviour.

"No; no one should touch you," she insisted.

Leaving George for a year seemed impossible. Deep down, however, I knew what the therapist was saying was right. I needed separation. That's why women go to shelters, where the recommendation is no contact—if you have contact, you're more likely to back. But the fact is that women do go back anyway because it's what they know, and because they believe it will get better. I couldn't bring myself to go in the first place.[5]

In July, we attended the annual fundraiser for the Banff Centre, a wonderful, internationally renowned institution that fosters all forms of artistic expression. If you do a Google search for me and George, the picture that will most likely pop up is one often used in media stories about him and that was taken at that event. We're standing with our tablemates, all good friends, looking happy and healthy when we were anything but. It's a reminder of how easy it is to judge based on superficial impressions. I'm sure people look at that photo and see a bunch of rich people without a care in the world.

The next month, in August, all five of us traveled to New York City before the kids returned to school. We stopped first in Toronto because George had decided he wanted to invest in a junior league hockey team with a former colleague. I'd gotten to know this man and his wife after John was born, and we'd become good friends. George loved the idea of owning a team, one John could possibly play on.

We stayed in a condo at Toronto's Ritz Carlton Hotel that George had purchased in 2011. Technically, the condo was for business as AltaCorp had a Toronto office. George furnished it stylishly, with sleek, expensive furniture from Roche Bobois. I hated the excess and extravagance; spending $30,000 for a sofa wasn't the way I'd been raised. George had outfitted every detail of the condo—every knob, light, mirror, and soap dish. He also slept with the real estate agent and flipped the condo a year later.

---

5 One 2019 Statistics Canada report showed that 20% of women who went to shelters returned to live with their abusers. They had no other place to go.

The same day as we arrived in Toronto, George went to the office before he was scheduled to meet his friend. I took the kids to meet with the man's wife and their children, who were all the same age as mine, at their home. Isla played with their daughter and the boys went to explore the neighbourhood. The plan was for all of us meet up at the end of the day for dinner.

This woman was the "Real Housewife" mentor I never had. In fact, she was the person who had spilled red wine on me during my first date with George, and we had since become good friends. She led me to her outdoor pool and poured pink champagne, even though it was morning. Isla was having a great time splashing in the water. Meanwhile, I was on full alert, anticipating that George would text at any moment.

Almost on cue, my phone began to blow up with angry texts.

"Where the fuck are you?"

"He's an asshole. Leave right now."

I didn't know what was going on, but figured whatever it was had to be huge. I began to text the boys, who weren't responding. My situational irritable bowel syndrome kicked in. I raced upstairs to my host's beautiful bathroom, where I plugged the toilet, with water spilling over. I was horrified. It's one of those scenes that's funny later, but it was a nightmare at the time.

When the boys finally came back, we made our excuses and exited quickly, my champagne untouched. We returned to the condo and found George, livid. The hockey team had gone belly-up the day after he had cut a $250,000 cheque. He was angry because he had wanted to be involved in the team, but he had also valued the friendship, and felt it had been a huge betrayal.

That evening we went to the dinner that we were to have had with our friends. George refused to eat, and glared at me the entire meal. Afterward, we went to a Florence + the Machine concert, as planned, but George disappeared midway through the performance. I discovered him as I went to the bathroom—he was drinking alone. I tried to talk to him, but he was staring me down as if the hockey/betrayal situation was my fault.

On the tail of that fiasco, the family flew on to New York. That part of the trip started well, with a baseball game at Yankee Stadium, and the kids decked out in Yankee jerseys and hats. Isla loves musicals, so I got us all tickets to *The Book of Mormon*, *Avenue Q*, and *Venus Flytrap*. Things began to devolve at *The Book of Mormon*. George went to get us drinks and surreptitiously downed some vodka. At intermission, I confronted him about it. We had a reservation at a great restaurant, but I told him I was returning to the hotel instead. So, we all trooped back to the hotel.

Once there, George attacked me verbally in front of the kids, saying, "Your mom screwed around. We had the perfect family."

He then told them he needed to talk to me alone. We had two rooms, and they were in the other one. George then continued with his accusations, then threatened suicide once again. "I don't want to live," he said.

At some point John came in to check on us and decided I wasn't safe, so he brought the other two kids into our room. Isla immediately began walking around the room picking up whatever she thought was dangerous, like razors—anything that her eleven-year-old mind saw as risky.

"We all need to sleep," I told George, trying to contain the situation.

"I'm not sleeping with you," he said, and locked himself in the other room. I didn't think George should be alone, and decided John should stay with him to watch him. John agreed, which was a huge responsibility for a seventeen-year-old. We were scheduled to stay in New York for another two days, but I knew we had to leave. I booked an early flight for me and the children. George had not thought to cut off my credit cards—too much drinking.

As we were packing the next morning, George asked where we were going. "Home," I said. Seeing the lawyer had given me perspective and a little empowerment. I was finally setting the agenda a bit more. He wanted to come with us, he said, so we all ended up at the airport together.

A weird scene unfolded there. Sometimes when George and I fought, and he was drunk, he'd say he was going to leave me for a woman we knew in Calgary, a society type who was newly single. He had mentioned her in the hotel room the night earlier in front of the kids as his other option besides suicide. Guess who was at the gate for our Calgary flight? This woman, entirely by coincidence. "Your little buddy is over there," I told George, pointing at her. "Do you want me to get her number?" He found it funny, and our laughter took the edge off the moment. He apologized, and told me he loved me.

We returned to another round of couple's counselling. George asked a therapist he had met at Hoffman in California to stage a retreat with us at our house in the mountains. This generally isn't done, but George was persuasive. During this session, which included the therapist talking about her own failed marriage, George again expressed desire to make the marriage work. It seemed neither of us could fathom existing without the other. It was the "Not Me Without You" engraved on our wedding bands. That's the heart of trauma bonding. Neither of us felt any validity without the other.

It wasn't long after the retreat that George drunkenly tried to stab me in the kitchen. He was chopping vegetables and, as I walked by, he lashed out with a knife in his hand. Isla witnessed it. Later that week, George threw me up against a wall and choked me. Isla witnessed that too. But those would be the exceptions. After he beat me almost unconscious in Argentina, he did turn it around and become less physically violent toward me. Unfortunately, he instead became more violent toward himself. He began staying away from home day and night and, when he was with us, he seemed disconnected.

CHAPTER FOURTEEN

The Second Flood

THE SECOND FLOOD RIPPED through Calgary in the middle of June 2013, the worst the city had seen in almost a century. In 2005, it had rained for three weeks beforehand, so the flooding had been expected. This time, there had been only a little rain, so the onslaught came as a surprise. I received a call from George around 10 a.m. one day telling me to get everything out of our basement and first floor. He had been tipped by an engineer who worked for the city as to what was coming. With the boys helping, I got to work.

George had been in constant motion that spring, negotiating his next big deal. He was trying to buy the Phoenix Coyotes, an ailing National Hockey League team. Owning an NHL franchise had been a childhood dream of George's, and he was determined to make it happen. That entailed a lot of travel between Toronto and Phoenix. When he was in Calgary, he would sometimes stay with me.

I had decided not to follow my lawyer's advice and formally separate, and hadn't called her again. She was still in touch with me a year after my appointment, however, and offered to return my retainer. I told her to keep it because it made me feel safe, a sort of insurance policy. Meanwhile, George and I could still sleep together and even sometimes have sex despite everything we had been through. That probably said more about our ability to function with trauma than the true state of our relationship.

The water levels were peaking by 10 p.m. on the first night of the flood, so we evacuated with the children to the Hyatt downtown. But the flood was inundating downtown as well, and when everybody was evacuated from the Hyatt, we checked into the Blackfoot Inn, further away from the flooding. It took about a week for the water to recede to the point where we could return to the neighbourhood.

As he did during the previous flood, George took on a leadership role. He stayed at a friend's house and the two of them monitored the situation from close range. The crisis of the flood reduced the crisis levels in the Gosbee household as the "tribe" instinct kicked in again. We functioned as a family unit, with George as the spokesperson. Our house had been submerged by the waters of the Elbow River, and people came off the street to help as we ripped out drywall and demolished damaged parts of our house. It was hard work, and there was no time to wonder about George's moods.

The 2013 flood was larger, and affected many more people, than the first one. Among those hardest hit were those who lived along the river, where the most expensive real estate was. The loss of those homes caused financial problems and a great deal of stress for our family personally, and for many others. After the flood, Alberta premier Alison Redford said the province would buy destroyed homes at their assessed values; she planned to clear the floodways of housing and make parks or public spaces in their stead.

Our house, now condemned, had an assessed value of around $7 million, thanks in part to George having purchased an adjacent lot with plans to build a house extension. Along the way, however, he had decided we couldn't afford the new wing. A paved sports court was put on the lot instead. In July, soon after the flood, George gave the *Globe and Mail* a tour of the remains of our home. The article described George as a "prominent Calgary businessman" and photographed him in a white cowboy hat. "Inside a flood-ravaged, uninhabitable Calgary home," said the headline. I read a couple of meanings into "uninhabitable."

We packed up everything that survived the flood and I moved with the boys to our place in the mountains. I dropped Isla off to attend the National Ballet School's summer program in Toronto. I returned to the mountains to unpack all the boxes and wash the river debris off every kitchen utensil, pot, pan, and plate. George mostly stayed at Le Germain.

Negotiations to acquire the Coyotes had continued during that time, and were complicated and bumpy. There was a setback when big investors George had partnered with backed out at the last minute. He was devastated, but didn't give up. In response, he formed a company—Gozco—with an anonymous silent partner who contributed most of the funds. The deal apparently involved taking on a lot of debt. After a great deal of back and forth, Gozco and a bunch of other partners finally bought the team in August 2013 for US$170 million.

Because Gozco was the largest of the many shareholders, and George was the public face of Gozco, although not its biggest investor, he was named an NHL governor. That put him at the table for the league's annual meetings and made him an important person in the world of professional hockey: he was thrilled. But his appointment quickly became a point of conflict with the other investors, who resented George's propensity to steal the spotlight. They saw George as someone who was receiving the profile and the accolades without having invested the most money.

I was curious as to where George got the money to invest in the Coyotes, because he was always complaining about how broke he was. Hard as it may be to believe, the fortune George had made on the sale of his company in 2009 had seriously shrunk in size. Some of those funds had gone into AltaCorp Capital, some into failed investments. George had gone on a real estate binge, which included the expensive condo in Toronto, and there had been a lot of wild spending in general. We were personally down to maybe $10 million, as far as I could guess, and much of that was committed. That meant George was always worried about money, despite having earned more than most people can dream of.

When I asked George more than once how he could afford to buy into the Coyotes, he'd just look at me: "You are so stupid. Don't you listen?"

Sometimes when I asked, he'd throw me a bone: "The Coyotes are asking for $2 million."

"Could you give that to me in terms of the whole picture?" I'd ask.

"Why?" he'd answer. "You don't even understand it. I've told you this. You're stupid and can't remember."

He never did explain the details of the transaction to me. Whenever I raised the topic, the conversation became tense and the abuse would fly, so I backed off, again picking my fights.

The family needed somewhere to live in Calgary. George bought a house in the Aspen community, close to the kids' schools and a twenty-minute drive from our old house. The plan was to live there until the fate of our Elbow Park house was determined. Once again, I didn't see the house before George bought it. He picked it from three that were for sale on a high ridge.

George hated that house from the outset or, rather, he hated what it represented: failure. Elbow Park was one of the most prestigious neighbourhoods in the city, with large lots, old trees and a homogenous community of affluent people, most of whom belonged to The Glencoe, a private country club. Aspen is high density, with few trees and small lots, and further from downtown. We couldn't afford to buy in Elbow Park, or in Mount Royal, where many of our peers had moved, but George's spin was that we chose Aspen to be closer to the kids' schools.

I was happy about the move because I wanted out of our old community, in which I was still Hester Prynne. My relations with some of our neighbours were rocky, and I had very few people who supported me or who I felt I could turn to for advice or solace. The new house was smaller than the old house, but that was an advantage in my view. It had an open-plan kitchen with a family room off it that served as a central hub. That space brought us closer together as a family, both physically and emotionally. Our Elbow Park house had been so big that we could all exist without crossing paths.

George was still trying to recoup money from the government over the Elbow Park property. There'd be times where he would call me up and say, "This is devastating. The property value has dropped. We'll be lucky if we get $3 million for both lots." We ended up in a running fight with the province over whether we qualified for the buyout.

George's main focus, however, was hockey. Owning the Coyotes suddenly gave him a big profile. It also allowed him to start a new life, at least for himself, in Arizona. He rented a five-bedroom house in Phoenix that had been designed by the popular firm of Oz Architects in Scottdale, Arizona, who were famous for their rustic farmhouse designs.

Being physically separated from George so much of the time allowed me to gain some perspective and gave me time to work on myself and my relationships with my kids. I started reading A Course in Miracles, a self-study program based in spiritual psychotherapy created by Dr. Helen Schucman in the 1970s. The course, in short, is a way to train your mind to replace a thought system based on fear with one based on love. I'd been marinating in fear for years: fear of not being a good enough wife or mother, fear of having no control over my life, fear that someone else was writing my story, fear of not finding a fulfilling purpose in life. And I was literally living in fear for my safety.

I had a lot to feel positive about—my children, my family, and some friends who stuck with me, especially—but I was slowly coming to understand that no amount of thought-training was going to make me less fearful unless I changed my circumstances. Yes, I had put the divorce lawyer off, but that did not mean I thought our marriage was sustainable. I was also starting to realize that my expectations for George were unrealistic. Just because my mother had healed, it did not mean he would.

CHAPTER FIFTEEN

Turning Point

I GOOGLED "CLOSEST AL-ANON MEETING" on a Tuesday morning in May of 2014. Al-Anon isn't for addicts: it's for family members living with a person who has addiction problems. I'd known about it since I was young. I knew that my life had to change, and making the call was a small admission that I couldn't do it alone.

Even though George had been mostly in Arizona or travelling for business since the Coyotes purchase—Sochi, Russia, for the Olympic Games in February, and Norway in April—the rages and the blaming were still happening, mostly via text or phone now. He hurled the usual insults, although now he was also referring to me, mockingly, as "Einstein." He'd relay his obsession with X, saying that he had dreams about him.

I'd cut him off when the conversation went in those dark directions, but I remained tethered to George. In April, back in Calgary, he called in hysterics while I was out shopping with the kids. He'd tried to kill himself, he said, by running the car engine in the garage with the door closed. He'd fallen asleep, then woke up when he'd urinated on himself. Later, he denied it happened, but when I went home and checked his car, I smelled urine. A month later, he said something about having two bullets left. He'd dangle vague threats like that before me to instill fear, as he'd done in the past. Again, I cut him off. I tried to talk to him the next day about it, but he just mimicked me.

I felt cornered in these situations. If I talked and explained myself, he would become angry. If I listened and nodded, he'd become angry because I wasn't talking. The one thing that was clear was that I had a lot more power when I listened because I was in control of my own actions. And, on the whole, listening seemed to make George calmer as well.

Walking into the Al-Anon meeting in the basement of the Good Shepherd Church, I was terrified. I scoped out the room, about twenty-eight people, with fewer than five men. Their average age looked to be around seventy. I'd had therapists and friends who'd rejected the concept of twelve-step programs, but X had attended Al-Anon for a year and said it helped him. I was now motivated to give it a try.

Al-Anon's start dates to 1939, four years after Alcoholics Anonymous was founded. At that time, families of people in AA had started meeting informally and were following their own version of AA's famous twelve steps. Al-Anon became an official organization 1951, founded by Anne B. and Lois Wilson, the wife of AA co-founder Bill Wilson. They recognized that addiction is a disease that touches every member of the family, as well as the friends of the person addicted. These people face their own trauma and need support and resources, too.

People get AA and Al-Anon mixed up. I found the best description of the difference in an essay by Shari Albert: "In AA, the substances are drugs and alcohol. In Al-Anon, the substances are people, places, and situations." As she puts it: "Al-Anon is about one thing: YOU. Your actions, your history, your perspective, and your shit."

The chapter I visited had been operating since the 1950s. The woman who had founded it still ran it at the age of ninety-three. The first thing I learned walking in was the commitment required. "You need to attend at least six more meetings," the woman who greeted me told me.

I don't know if I can do that, I thought to myself. I figured I could just do the twelve steps on my own. Looking back, that assumption was incredibly arrogant of me, and common among newcomers.

A big part of Al-Anon is sitting around a circle sharing experiences and hopes. Going around the first time, I critiqued everyone in my head. It was defensive, something you do when you're frightened.[6]

Al-Anon is not the answer for everyone but, for me, it became an anchor. It helped me understand the family dynamics that accompany addiction. The family can become complicit in the problem by covering for the addict, attempting to protect him or her and the family's "reputation." Family members also have their own issues and their own recovery processes that entail loss, grieving, understanding, and forgiveness.

When I spoke to George about Al-Anon, I sensed he was threatened by it but he didn't discourage me from going. The meetings forced me to look at the reality of George's addiction and helped me understand dimensions of that addiction that had been mysterious to me. It taught me how high-risk behaviours and sexual deviance are often part of the addiction cycle, which can include porn addiction.

Even before the internet, George used a lot of pornography, keeping stacks of magazines like *Hustler*. Throughout our marriage, he had been preoccupied with the idea of me having sex with a man while he watched, but I had managed a steadfast "no." After my affair, these requests were less frequent. Whatever thrill that fantasy held for him was diminished, probably because the affair had been my choice, and the power dynamic had changed. And, after the affair, his porn obsession took on a new, disturbing focus: I would catch him watching porn with blonde women having sex with black men.

Through Al-Anon, I also gained insight into what was going on with my life. I began to see how my immediate family was abetting George by keeping up appearances. I came to a better understanding of the connection

---

6 Writing or talking about Al-Anon is taboo. Like AA, the organization adheres to strict confidentiality rules. These rules are vital for providing a safe space where people can tell their story without judgment and with unconditional support. I respect the need to protect confidences and identities, but I question the secrecy in terms of not being allowed to discuss the personal benefits. I also think it reinforces the code of silence that still shrouds addiction. We give a lot of lip service to removing "stigma," but to do that we need to speak openly without fear of judgment, or a sense that somehow we have failed.

between addiction and abuse. The book *How Al-Anon Works for Families & Friends of Alcoholics* features the section "A Special Word to Anyone Confronted by Violence," in which violence is recognized as part of the addiction dynamic. It's not a topic that we otherwise discuss openly.

I met my Al-Anon sponsor in an unusual manner. I had attended for about six months when the ninety-three-year-old woman who had founded the chapter barreled toward me on her walker, hooked up to an oxygen tank: "We're going to start working on your steps," she announced. She asked me if I was depressed, adding that she suspected so because I never wore bright colors and didn't participate much.

That is typically not the way Al-Anon works. One of the mottos is "You don't impose, you don't approach." The idea is that a person must cultivate the confidence to participate on their own. But my sponsor seemed to sense that wasn't going to work with me, and her approach was a blessing in disguise. I probably wouldn't have stepped up on my own because, while eager to begin, I remained frightened and judgmental.

Getting to know people who'd lived for decades with drug- and alcohol-dependent relatives also forced me to see my future. Growing old with an addict is hard. Their partners often wind up voiceless, exhausted, and prematurely aged.

One woman in particular was a cautionary tale for me. The first time I saw her, she was telling her story while her husband, an old cowboy type, watched from the sidelines. I sensed she was on heightened alert, speaking softly, careful with every word, reading his bodily responses to her story and the questions she got afterwards. Would there be consequences when she got home? I saw so many similarities to my own dynamic with George that it was chilling. She began by saying that her husband did not have the disease "like everyone else." He could be sober and in the program for ten to fifteen years and then relapse to addictive behaviour, followed once again by sobriety. What kept her sane was her commitment to Al-Anon. She said it saved her life. There was little doubt in my mind that her husband was abusive, and that her only refuge was Al-Anon. I realized how easily I could be her, worried that she was offending "her alcoholic" (that's how Al-Anon describes those with substance addictions, as if we own them).

Al-Anon provided me with other practical tools. One of its central tenets is "Keep looking after yourself and being the best you can be." And I began to follow its advice for dealing with crises: "Don't fight with them. Don't engage." Instead, you are to "detach with love." You have to learn to create boundaries. You don't put your own skin in the game. You say, "You might be right, dear."

I was encouraged to keep out of harm's way and not think that I had to resolve every situation. Not stepping in and solving someone else's problem allows them to grow while at the same time letting you protect yourself. We were told, "No matter what seems to trigger the attack, we all deserve to be safe." I was advised to keep a separate set of car keys for emergency escapes, and to make sure I had access to a "safe house."

Important as it was to me, I wasn't ready to fully accept what I was hearing at Al-Anon. Change is a process: often a slow one. I still hadn't entirely let go of thinking that I could solve George, that there was a magical solution to his problems. I finished the twelve steps within the first few years, and part of that is learning the act of forgiveness: to ask for forgiveness, and to forgive as well. Of course, I asked George for forgiveness and apologized for my affair and being unkind to him. I was sincere in that, but one has to work at forgiveness daily. Forgiveness only occurs when behaviours and attitudes change and, again, for me, it was a process.

Those qualifiers notwithstanding, Al-Anon had a positive impact on me. I felt more self-reliant, which made me happier. I can see it in retrospect when I reread my journals. I was working to stop behaviours I could see were petty and mean. Everything didn't need to be perfect, and I was getting better at tolerating imperfection. "You waste too much time getting your way," I wrote. Better to be respectful and kind.

As I changed, my responses to George's behaviour changed, and that affected the equilibrium of the relationship. In June, we went as a family to the NHL awards in Las Vegas. At the dinner, George drank alcohol in front of the kids and me, sparkling water with vodka. He told me later he hated how boring our life had become. He missed our old peer group, the community, the life we didn't have anymore because of me, he said. Then he told me he wanted to have exhibitionistic sex in the window of our hotel room. It was something he might have been able to bully me into before. I refused and went to bed at 10 p.m.

Al-Anon expanded my understanding of co-dependence, a concept that comes out of AA and remains contentious in psychology. Co-dependence recognizes that family and friends might actually interfere with recovery by over-helping. We become as addicted to the drinker as the drinker is to alcohol, and we, too, can become ill. When someone told me years earlier that I was co-dependent because I'd grown up with alcoholism, I denied it. Yet I had a constant reminder of what co-dependence was literally inscribed on my ring finger: "Not me without you."

George gave me a sense of "me," of self-definition. I believed I couldn't exist without him, even while my existence with him was one of constant stress, fear, and belittlement. I had become such a by-product of who he was that I lost sight of myself. When George was mad or giving me the silent treatment, I almost felt like I needed a "fix," by which I mean him telling me things would be okay and, just like that, I'd feel better. If we hadn't fought for a long time, I would start to get antsy, expecting—indeed know-ing—that another shoe would soon drop. I was totally wired for George.

It took me a long time to see how harmful this was: that I was reinforc-ing the very thing I needed to change, and that I had to wean myself off this behaviour. The Boston-based Dutch psychiatrist and pioneering PTSD researcher Bessel van der Kolk has done important research on trauma. In his work, he explains how, contrary to what we might think, a climate of fear and terror can increase the need for attachment, even if the source of that comfort is harmful.

Understanding co-dependency forced me to address questions I'd always had about my marriage. Like, why George? What made him so attractive to me? When I finally understood co-dependency and addiction, I could see it. Part of me craved the drama and the trauma. I was so accustomed to being on the edge that my body would actually get sore when the trauma slowed.

My children began going to therapy in 2011, after the police were called to the house. George agreed to that because the social worker who had investigated the family after the incident had made it clear it was non-negotiable. John and Carter went together, but had separate sessions as one waited for the other. I wanted them to have a male with whom they could develop healthy older male relationships. I took Isla to her sessions. I always tried to speak openly to my kids about what was going on and, in time, I'd tell them about my own childhood and my mother's suicide attempt. The therapist objected to this, saying they didn't need to know. I disagreed. I didn't want my children to have their family history swept under the rug the way it had been for me.

I understand many people on the outside will say, "Oh my God, she exposed them to too much!" My counter-argument is that if I hadn't given the kids the ability to talk openly, they wouldn't have learned to understand the emotions they were experiencing. I wanted to have open discussions about drug addiction and binge drinking. I wanted it as open as possible. "Truth and alcohol is an oxymoron," I wrote in my journal. "They can't coexist."

One therapist said that what I was committing "emotional incest," a term thrown around a lot to describe a type of abuse where a parent looks to a child for the sort of emotional support normally provided by another adult. It's a common pattern in diseased families, and is often seen in cases of divorce or families where one parent has a substance addiction. This therapist in particular was concerned that Isla was being exposed to too much.

"You can't hide this from her," I said.

"You could say nothing," she suggested.

Again, that wasn't an option for me: "If you don't talk, it's just more secrecy."

Her concern was that Isla couldn't process what I was exposing her to. "She has to process this," I told her. As the therapist was speaking, I realized she didn't understand the dynamics of a household with ongoing violence and abuse. I thought: *Well, you live my life, and have your kids exposed to the things my kids have been exposed to, and see if you feel comfortable not having that conversation with them.* I knew from my own childhood how damaging it was when people weren't open. Children intuit when something is amiss, and silence only reinforces their anxiety. I'd gotten a glimpse into my own family's ongoing pattern of denial when I travelled with George to the Scripps Clinic in 2003. The clinic needed a family medical history

from each of us, so I got my doctor dad to fill it out for me. He listed diseases like cancers, but the mental health section was left blank. I asked him
why. "The family hasn't had any problems with mental health," he told me.
I couldn't believe it. Our family had been ravaged by my mother's depression and suicide attempt, but it was still something we didn't talk about,
even to professionals.

I recommend therapy to anyone in emotional turmoil, but the relationship between a therapist and patient is a delicate one. It is crucial to be
twinned both with the right person and with the right therapy for the right
problem. Therapists have a lot of influence on people who are vulnerable.
The sad thing is that very few people have any access at all to publicly funded
therapy, and most women in abusive relationships are more occupied with
meeting their basic needs—food, shelter, safety, medical care—than seeing
therapists.[7]

Going to Al-Anon inspired me to learn more about mental illness and
addiction more generally. I found a continuing education course in addiction studies and enrolled in part out of interest, but part of it was the
growing recognition that my children only had me as a role model, and thus
it was up to me to demonstrate good behaviour for them. I was particularly
concerned about Carter, my most independent and rebellious child, who
had been losing interest in school. If he saw me studying, I thought, it might
inspire him as well.

It may seem like a small thing but, given more than a decade of ridicule
of hearing how stupid I was, taking a course was a big step for me. The
course was useful in providing a good overview of mental health and addiction. It also opened my eyes to the lack of resources for addicted individuals,
especially since I was attending Al-Anon at the same time.

George did not like that I was taking the course. He was scrambling,
sensing his control over me was lessening. He agreed, once again, to see a

---

7   For more on the lack of publicly funded therapy, see "Physician psychotherapy unavailable to
    ninety-seven percent of people with urgent mental health needs in Ontario" by the Centre of
    Addiction and Mental Health, 11 March, 2020. https://www.camh.ca/en/camh-news-and-stories/
    psychotherapy-unavailable-people-urgent-mental-health-needs-ontario

therapist but as 2014 progressed, his rages and threats to commit suicide continued. He was focused on money. We were in "financial ruin," he'd say, this time because of a huge tax bill related to the purchase of the Coyotes. That made no sense to me, given that George had most recently said we'd only put $1 million into the deal.

Our flood-damaged Elbow Park property continued to be problematic. The house had been condemned back in the summer of 2013, but still nothing was happening with the provincial buyout. There were big changes in the provincial government that spring and summer, and the rules around the buyout were changing. There were disagreements about whether or not our home was actually on the flood plain, and we no longer knew if we would even qualify for the buyout. George was furious. In July, after taking a few Ambien, he became belligerent and accused me of sleeping with my brother-in-law.

I asked again, gently, about our finances. "I'm sure there's something I don't know," I wrote in my journal in August.

I sensed we were in deep debt. One minute, he would say we were okay; the next, it was "you have no idea." His story was always changing, but the message generally was bad. He apparently had told his parents we were flat broke. He would tell me, repeatedly, that he'd get us out of debt, make some money for me, then blow his head off. This terrified me, but I was also becoming accustomed to his threats.

By late 2014, the Canadian buyers of the Coyotes, including George, realized that they needed an American as a majority shareholder to solve their tax problems. And so, in October 2014, the hedge-fund manager Andy Barroway bought fifty-one percent of the team. George was still involved but he stepped down as governor, a role he had loved.

In retrospect, I can see more clearly that George was in a downward spiral. He was more manic. In the fall, he had his second hair transplant surgery and traveled to Boston to see Derek Jeter play his last game for the Yankees. He desperately needed to be able to say "I was there." When he traveled to China that September, he had a psychotic episode—something that had happened before. He told me he was being tied up in his bed. When he returned, he had an episode where he was sweating profusely, and thought it was a heart attack. The day after, he told me he wanted to have sex. In the past, I would have appeased him. This time I didn't. I realized I was sick of the dynamic.

CHAPTER SIXTEEN

Black Christmas

CHRISTMAS DAY 2014, George was in a rage. What had set him off first thing in the morning was the sight of wrapped gifts I'd bought for a close friend of his who lived in Singapore. George knew I'd bought them, but at that moment he'd clearly forgotten. He immediately jumped to the conclusion that I was having an affair with this male friend—I'd always got along with him better than George did.

I tried to diffuse the situation. I told George to open the gifts. He angrily unwrapped them to find two sterling silver tooth-fairy boxes for his friend's new twins. That didn't end his anger. "You're still fucking around," he yelled. "I can't trust you." He stormed off to bed for a while.

The tension continued later as the family opened gifts. I monitored George's reactions, as I always did, fighting back tears. Halfway through breakfast, George went back to bed again. The boys went out to play hockey, and Isla and I went to visit my parents, who were then living in Calgary.

My dad was recovering from eye surgery, and we had all agreed to get together for Christmas. I told George to let me know if he wanted to organize something with his parents, which he did, and he agreed to prepare Christmas dinner, something he'd done many times before and enjoyed.

Thanks to Al-Anon, I was not trying to manage everyone and everything. Still, habits are hard to shake. On my way to see my parents, I called George's mom and dad to say that dinner was not happening because George was still in bed.

While Isla and I were playing cribbage with my family, a stream of "Goodbye Karen" texts from George began pinging on my phone: "Great knowing you," one said. "Tell people I loved them."

Immediately, I knew something was off. The messages were filled with references to "self-sacrifice" lifted from the television series *Marco Polo*, which George was binge-watching on Netflix. The messages were barely coherent, but extreme and worrying. He talked about "sacrificing myself to free Marco Polo." Other messages were garbled: "I dhdndksyou dknt wanajd kicjdbe by karns." The children and I were used to receiving messages like this when George was drinking, but his incoherence in a suicidal context worried me.

I phoned George's parents, who were by then at our house: they had decided to check on him. His mother sounded upbeat. They'd put the turkey in, she said, and it smelled fabulous. They'd seen and talked to George and everything was great.

That didn't square with George's texts. I knew it was bullshit, and that there was no use talking candidly to George's mother. She didn't want to hear it. Notwithstanding Al-Anon's instructions to back off, I knew I needed to get home.

Isla and I arrived just after the boys returned home as well. I ran upstairs to find George in bed, curled into a fetal position under the covers, and completely out of it. He mumbled something about saying good-bye to me once again, and I went to kiss him so I could smell how liquored up he was. As I did, I was overwhelmed instead by the smell of blood: that metallic, acrid odour you can almost taste. I tore the sheets away to see he was lying in a pool of it. He had stabbed himself with a small chef's knife his mom and dad had given him for Christmas. Later, he told me it was an act of self-sacrifice of the kind they did during the Yuan Dynasty—that explained his references to *Marco Polo*.

I ran to the top of the stairs and called for his father, who was a physician, to please come up: that that George had attempted suicide, and I was calling 911. "Please look at him," I said. This is how dysfunctional the situation had become: I wasn't only worried about George's health. I was so used to being blamed that I felt the need to document that George had done this on his own. I was afraid his parents would try and deny the situation or cover it up or somehow hold me responsible.

In the ambulance on the way to Calgary's Foothills Medical Centre, one of the paramedics turned to me in surprise. "You don't seem that shocked," he said. I suppose I felt frozen rather than shocked. The paramedic didn't know how many times George had threatened to harm himself, and how many years I'd lived with the fear that this, or worse, would happen.

The minute we got to the ER, George was put in triage. The medical staff needed to keep him there until they could put him into an observation room and determine how much of a danger he was to himself and the people around him. Toxicology screens revealed both alcohol and sleeping pills in George's system, and so they also needed to wait until the drugs wore off to assess his psychiatric condition. Would he express remorse? Would he know the consequences of what he had done? These are the sort of things that determine whether a person will be admitted to the psychiatric ward.

Fortunately, he had not damaged any major organs. George was still drunk but becoming alert. I waited at least five to six hours to hear if he'd be admitted, and during that time, George drifted in and out of lucidity. "When you dine with the premier's wife of China, please remember to wear red," he said. At another point he asked, "You had a good Christmas, though? I got you a really nice purse, it's Prada." I'd nod and agree.

Other times, he'd wake angry. "I hate you, this is all your fault," he told me. Or he'd panic: "I can't live. People can't find out about this." He was terrified about being put in a psychiatric ward; my main concern was that he'd be released. I didn't think I could give him the help he needed at home.

I finally went home around three in the morning to get some sleep, still not knowing whether George would be admitted. I fell to my knees and prayed. I prayed for George, the family, and for me. I prayed that we would have the strength to get through the coming days, and that I would have the guidance to make the right decisions.

The next day was Boxing Day, and because it was the holidays, it would be December 29 before there was a psychiatrist who could release George. Consequently, George spent several days in the psychiatric ward. I told the on-call psychiatrist that George wanted to go to rehab, and asked where his chances would be best. He stared at me blankly. "Your husband is a drunk and it doesn't matter which rehab he goes to," he said. "It is only up to him to decide if he wants to get better."

The psychiatrist's blunt assessment reinforced my growing sense that I wasn't going to be able to help George with his recovery—it was completely up to him. I stopped researching rehab centers. As they said at Al-Anon, "Let go and let God. If he wants to get better, he'll get better. You can't do it for him."

Here I need to say something about record keeping and consistency. After someone has been to ER, their medical records go back to their primary care doctor. Every time George went to ER, say for a panic attack, he'd say he didn't have a doctor because he didn't want a paper trail. I felt it important that his doctor know what was going on, so I'd make sure the hospital knew: "His doctor is so-and-so, and make sure he gets it." When George left the psychiatric unit, he wanted no record of ever being there. The nurse assured him he could take his report with him, and George thought he was out of the system. He decided that he'd go to Sierra Tucson, in Arizona, for rehab after his release, and I did the same with his records from rehab. I copied them and brought them to George's regular physician. "I'm not reporting him," I'd say, "but it's important you know this is happening with his health."

When George decided to go to Sierra Tucson, I began to check it out, to make sure it was the best place for him, before catching myself: "You can't do it for him," I repeated to myself.

George entered treatment on January 1, 2015, for four weeks. He told everyone that he had to spend a month in hospital for a stomach condition, and he wouldn't be permitted visitors. He told the kids to say the same thing to anyone who asked. George's parents were also adamant that no one know. I later found out that, in the minutes after the paramedics had taken George to emergency, they had taken my children's phones away and told the kids they were not to tell anyone what had happened for the sake of the family and for George's reputation. Isla, who was very upset, called my mother, with whom she's close, to tell her what had happened. My mother and father went to the house right away.

The family culture was all secrecy and white-washing, and that environment wasn't helping George confront his problems. Avoidance and denial only perpetuate problems. I understood the impulses. In the past, I would have removed any evidence of George's attempted suicide. This time, however, I didn't. I left the blood stain on the box spring as a constant reminder.

CHAPTER SEVENTEEN

Money and Control

BEFORE GEORGE WENT INTO REHAB, I did something I'd never done: I demanded access to our accounts, both email and online banking. We'd always had a joint banking account but, since 2002, only George and his assistant had managed it. I could only withdraw and look at balances. I gathered we had money problems, but I never had enough information to know how big or what kind.

George, at first, rejected my demand. Our finances were too complicated for me to understand, he told me.

"Okay, explain it," I said. He used the question to shut discussion down, and belittle me.

"How many times do I need to explain this?" he'd say.

When I persisted in asking for control, he agreed to give me partial control over email. I would share the account with him and his assistant. He also said I would have control of the bank accounts, but he never delivered on that one.

I had come to realize, with the help of my Al-Anon sponsor, that my personal financial situation was precarious. I had no credit rating, and no credit card of my own with which to build one. It's difficult to stand on your own without credit. So, after a big fight with George, I got a credit card in my own right, just to run a balance of $80 a month and pay it off to establish my credit.

Around that time, Isla helped me gain control over my email. Being thirteen years old, she was far more tech savvy than either of her parents. She figured out how George accessed my computer and phone from his computer, and how his assistant could log into my account and read my emails. She blocked their access. She also figured out how to pinpoint George's location, even to the point of being able to access his texts, although I didn't learn about this until later on and, in retrospect, Isla shouldn't have been involved at all. The pattern of saving and fixing, the perception of control over someone else, was clearly passed on to her through George and myself. She has since gone to therapy specifically for this reason.

It was impossible to block his assistant out of my email account entirely because George was the primary account holder, and he had put her name on the account. Sometimes I would be alerted to George accessing my account remotely because the password would be changed from what I had set it to, but that was happening less now. George was increasingly wrapped up in his life down south.

There was one unexpectedly positive and important development in our home during this time. While George was away at Sierra Tucson for the month of January, we added a new member to the household: Marc Hoff, a German exchange student who went to school and played hockey with John. Without asking me, George told Marc he could live with us. Initially I was angry about it. Between the flood and moving, and taking care of George and the children and the dogs, I was exhausted. I had done all of the physical work while George was buying the Coyotes in Arizona.

But Marc's arrival proved an unexpected godsend. He is a terrific young man who was great to have around. His presence also meant George never became aggressive toward me or touched me after he returned from rehab. Perception was everything to George. He was always well-behaved in front of Marc, an outsider with intel to the Gosbees' inner world. I'd come to call Marc "my guardian angel."

Any gains George made at rehab were short-lived. Part of his recovery protocol on returning home was to attend weekly AA meetings, but he chose not to. He didn't need AA, he said. He claimed not to believe in the program. He also worried about how not drinking would affect his ability to do business in an industry fueled by socializing around alcohol. I noticed that he'd regularly be out of town Mondays so that he would miss meetings. When someone is committed to AA's 12-step recovery program, they never miss a meeting—even when it's in another language. People go for the fellowship, the energy in the room that helps them find the strength to remain sober, which is also true for Al-Anon. They fear that if they disrupt their commitment, there's room for relapse. It quickly became clear that George was not committed to AA, or to his recovery.

Most weeks, George was in Phoenix Monday to Friday. Then he'd call on Friday to say he wanted to stay: "It's so nice here."

"So stay," I'd tell him.

Calgary winters are cold and long, but that wasn't the reason I was glad he stayed in Arizona. I knew the children and I were safer with him at a distance. "How can we be safe? How can we be safe? How can we be safe?" I asked myself in my journal.

When George was back in Calgary, we lived in a state of constant tension —the smallest thing would trigger an eruption. In March, I turned off the alarm clock, which meant he didn't make it to a yoga class. He flew into a rage, telling me I had the emotional and intellectual capacity of an infant. Still, somehow, we kept up the outer veneer of a united family. I did travel down to Arizona with George a few times, once when the hockey team's coach, Dave Tippett, wanted to meet me and introduce me to his wife, who was a realtor. George told me to look at some houses with her to create the perception that we were all going to move to Arizona: again, "perception is everything." He wanted the fans to have some assurance that the owners were permanent. I believe he also wanted to communicate that he could afford to buy a house on the spot.

Meanwhile, I was also being told that George's reputation in Arizona was not that of a family man. He was a regular at a club where everyone would ask if he was single. When George was being hostile, he'd tell me he knew many women in Arizona were interested in him, and that I was lucky that he wanted to continue to try with the marriage.

It was also becoming apparent to me that George was not well physically. "There is something very wrong with him," I wrote in my journal.

And no wonder: he was on a diet of escitalopram, disulfiram (better known as Antabuse), and naltrexone hydrochloride. The HGH, combined with the drugs and with the booze I suspected he was drinking, gave him an engorged and angry look. He once blew his nose and blood gushed out. I also found a bottle of vodka he had stashed when packing to go to Vernon, B.C., for a hockey tournament Carter was playing in.

George's addictions weren't just to substances: they included shopping and spending. George burned through money on trips, clothing, gadgets—anything that offered a status boost. He had closets full of running shoes, dress shoes, hiking books, shooting boots. He would order still more new pairs of boots and, if they didn't fit, he'd just order another pair without returning them. He had enough camouflage hunting and bone-fishing out-fits to last a lifetime, although he only went bone-fishing a couple of times. He was completely outfitted for extreme mountain and ice climbing, with all the down jackets and cold-weather suits and ice picks, ice books, com-puters and satellite phones and portable printers, tents, and freeze-dried food. He would become obsessed with buying particular items like garbage disposals, and would order five to figure out which had the best design. Things were delivered every day for him: an oxygen chamber, a sous vide kitchen appliance, an entire china collection, headphones, a huge selec-tion of white lights for seasonal affective disorder. His assistant at Altacorp Capital was nicknamed Shipping-and-Receiving.

Around this same time period, George added yet another addiction to his list, but one that's socially sanctioned, even admired: he was determined to scale the world's highest peaks. He'd always liked risky sports such as heli-skiing in the Rockies, but this new direction was next level: a manifes-tation of his belief he was a superman who could conquer all of his demons through force of will.

It was obvious that we were drifting further and further apart, spend-ing less and less time together, but divorce still wasn't in the picture. I did that voodoo math and convinced myself that the situation was sustainable. I knew my central role was to care for and protect my kids, and to be a positive role model for them. As much as I was realizing that George's prom-ises of recovery would never come through, that his destructive behaviours would negate any kind of recovery or healing, and that I was the one need-ing to let go of those expectations, I couldn't bring myself to make the break. Even if George would never heal, I felt a certain responsibility for him given his depression and his addictions. He was mentally ill. Can you just abandon someone who is mentally ill? I debated this in my journal. I'd vowed "In sickness and in health." Was it okay to just move on?

Back and forth I went. I loved him and wanted him to be healthy, but his illness had also infected me to the point that it consumed my life. When he was given a choice, he chose (or was attracted to) drinking, sneaking sleeping pills, and not going to AA. In one journal entry, I was candid: "He is killing me, he is really killing the life out of me."

As time passed, I leaned more toward a break: "I need to leave this man. He has overshadowed me for twenty-plus years. It is time for me to cut the cord."

It wasn't just an interior monologue telling me I had to leave. My thera-pist laid it on the line: "He isn't changing," she said. "What are you going to do?" And my family was also beginning to apply pressure: "Why are you staying?"

I was leaning toward leaving, and I was getting support to leave, but bringing myself to do it was a problem. I continued to think and read books like Tian Dayton's *The ACOA Trauma Syndrome: The Impact of Childhood Pain on Adult Relationships*. I couldn't put it down. It told me so much about my childhood and my relationship with George. "He is like my surrogate drunk mother that I am so attached to," I wrote in my diary in August.

I wasn't the only one struggling with what to do about George. His own family was torn about his addiction. His parents saw it and at the same time denied it, which is a common reaction in families.

On a vacation in Palm Desert, California, George forgot his sleeping pills back in Calgary, and was freaking out about it. I told him to get his mother, who was coming to join us, to bring them. "There's no way," he said, knowing his mother would say no. He told me to tell her. I got our housekeeper back in Calgary to put the pills in a pair of socks, and put the socks in one of my purses. I told his mother I needed the purse and the socks in the purse. When they arrived, she handed me the purse in front of my mom and dad who were visiting, too. "Karen, here's your purse," she said. "And your sleeping pills are in it."

"They're not mine," I said. "They're George's."

She didn't want to hear it.

In early 2015, I talked to his mom and dad about George. They asked how he was doing. "Frankly, I don't know," I said. "Everything is up in the air. He might have relapsed, and if he has, there's no way we can live together. He does not like me when he drinks." I told them we both had work to do.

George's father was sympathetic. "Karen you have tried for so long, I can understand."

His mother said she suspected he was drinking again, and asked, "Why do you stay with him?"

Then, without warning, they would flip. "Karen, what are you talking about? He's our son and he's awesome. There's no problem. George is fine, he's not drinking."

I became more systematic in how I dealt with George's abusive remarks, making a list of responses. I kept them in my car, in the kitchen, on my phone and folded up in my phone case:

> *I'm sorry you feel that way.*
> *I can accept your faulty perception of me that I'm different/being a bitch/*
>   *have conditions/angry, etc.*
> *I have no right to control how you see me.*
> *I guess I have to accept that's how you feel.*
> *Your anger is not my responsibility.*

And I kept this one uppermost in my mind: "The best way to deal with a narcissist is no contact at all." Not that I could manage it.

In May, George went to India for ten days with John, who'd just finished his freshman year in chemical engineering at Northeastern University in Boston. George saw it as a bonding trip and a spiritual journey. He had become interested in Eastern enlightenment, and wanted to be "holistic" about his recovery.

George needed to rebuild trust with each of our children, and I encouraged him to do it. At the same time, I feared the reconciliation wouldn't happen. "There is a black hole of trust that never will be filled," I wrote in my journal.

The trip to India didn't rebuild his relationship with John; instead, it went off the rails, although I didn't know it at the time. After a day of business, George appeared drunk on the way to dinner—John's first indication that his father might be drinking again. George and John were staying in separate rooms, and John wasn't able to make contact for almost a day. George told John that he had travel sickness and that was why he had been missing in action for so long. John was upset, feeling echoes of our past experiences with George. We later learned that a Calgary woman with whom George was involved had made the trip as well, which explained his absences.

It wasn't the creepiest behaviour John was exposed to when he was with his father, unfortunately. When they were together in Arizona, George would invite him to parties and point out younger women (whom George had found jobs for) in attendance. "She's interested in you," he would tell John, encouraging him to make a move. John suspected something was up but didn't say anything, or make any moves. It later turned out that George was involved with the young women he was encouraging John to interact with.

The rest of 2015 went on in this rocky fashion. Hostile texts came with the territory: "Hey Einstein, let's talk before you become the laughing stock once more. Still my money. Still my kids. Still my friends. Still your debt. We need 2 people to be smart. If one is really stupid, kids will suffer . . . I married one of the dumbest broads of all time and I tried to cover it up. I paid the price with my reputation. Now we are all going to pay the price with Your stupidity . . . Good luck Karen and thanks for fucking everyone's lives."

George continued to have psychotic incidents. He called one Saturday morning from China, where he'd had a similar, previous episode of going off the rails. I was in Grand Prairie for a hockey tournament with Carter, and answered to hear George was freak out: "Don't call the Embassy, but

I want you to know I'm okay," he said. "They're outside and have tied me to the bed but I'm going to be okay. They've tortured me and I'm hurt. I'm all beat up; you'll see when you see me." I hung up the phone, prayed he was safe, and went to Carter's hockey game that afternoon. But when he returned from China, he wouldn't discuss the matter.

I was becoming numb to both the insults and the psychotic episodes, although I did have a dream of flying to China to identify George's body and getting tangled up in the bureaucracy of bringing it home from China.

Meantime, the money problems continued. I went to Mexico with John and Isla and a couple of their friends. Before we left, I went to the bank to withdraw the Mexican equivalent of $2,000 American. The teller told me I couldn't. "The account is in the minuses," she said.

I called George. "What is going on?" I asked.

He jumped right to the offence. "That's why I don't want you to have access," he said. "You don't understand it and you stress me out and it will turn into a big thing." He then gave me a long story about how he had borrowed money at a lower rate, and was investing it at a higher rate, and that he'd pay the loan off in due time. He told me I was so fucking stupid to question all the things he was doing to maintain our lifestyle. The next day, however, his assistant drove to the house with US$2,000.

While we were in Mexico, George was supposed to go to Medicine Hat and Grande Prairie for hockey tryouts with Carter. He got two rooms at the hotel in Grande Prairie the first night: one for Carter and one for himself. That way he could drink freely before and after Carter's tryouts. The tryout for the Medicine Hat team was the more important one to make, but the night before the tryout, George got drunk and overslept the next morning. That meant Carter was late. Carter knew his father was drinking the entire time, but never told me. He believed he was protecting me. It breaks my heart now to think of the stress and anxiety he experienced. Carter's journal at the time of the Medicine Hat tryout (he gave me permission to share it) referred to his dad as "a fucking lying piece of drunkin shit because he knows he drinks and lies etc. it was awful."

In retrospect, it wasn't surprising Carter gave up playing hockey, a sport he loved, the next year. By this point, the effect of George's drinking on the children was becoming palpable. In August, Isla told me she related to the Tracy Chapman song "Fast Car," which was released in 1988, before George and I even met. She was referencing the part about the singer's father having a problem with the bottle, and his body being too old for working, and too young to look like it did.

My going to Mexico without George had been strategic. I had never booked a trip without his approval before, and without him joining us. I was taking baby steps toward my independence. I was starting to think about how I could support myself, and even possibly pay for the kids' educations, without him. I wanted to keep taking courses to bolster my confidence. I was feeling strong with the help of counselling, and finally realizing that I could accept responsibility for my behaviour and what I had done wrong in the marriage without deserving George's abusive treatment. Needing evidence to convince myself and others about the craziness of George's behaviour, I began keeping his raging texts, which would come in twelve-hour cycles.

I tried not to worry and think about George because I had no control over him—but, again, that was easier said than done. "Protect me Karen, Protect me Karen, Protect me Karen," I wrote in my journal. "I feel he hates me, never felt as strongly as now."

But, by the time Christmas 2015 rolled around, I was putting a happy gloss on things in my journal. We spent the holiday at our mountain house, the site of George's suicide attempt a year earlier. "We made it," I wrote. People were in good moods, I reported. George went to yoga in the afternoon and we had dinner at the Gosbees'. "I felt hope," I wrote. "I felt so lucky to be surrounded by my family, those who I love."

CHAPTER EIGHTEEN

Paris

GEORGE'S BEHAVIOUR THROUGH the holidays had put me back on the hope train as 2016 began. The major reason for my optimism was that he wasn't drinking. We were talking, and he was making an effort to connect with the children and me. As I noted in my journal, he even smelled different. "It is the closest to a miracle I have ever experienced," I wrote on January 14.

Two days later, the miracle was over. George had left on a trip to the U.S., and was sending hostile texts again. I would send George a note wishing him a good morning and a good day, asking how the weather was, and he'd respond with blistering hatred. "I don't want to be with you. I'm going to talk to my lawyer tomorrow. I'm sick of all this constant battle [to] meet all of your conditions and meet your approval. . . . You have done nothing but cause me pain. I have been doing awesome for months but it's not good enough. Just got to my hotel."

The best clue I'd have as to his state of mind would be if he used my name, Karen, in a text instead of "Einstein" or "idiot" or "you cunt."

In the spring, Isla was accepted to a summer course at the Paris Ballet School. George wanted to take her, and Isla pressed for it. "I want to do this, Mommy," she begged. George treated Isla like his little princess, a reinforcement she liked. My relationship with her was far more practical. I had my doubts and I told her I didn't think it was wise.

Isla was fourteen at the time. She was too young to be making decisions for herself. Some weeks before, George had appeared to be drinking in front of her in Arizona, in the Coyotes' owners' box. She had a hard time with it, and chose not to believe George was actually drinking. That's the way it is in a diseased family: you can virtually see and smell the alcohol but you doubt what was right in front of you. We all wanted to give George the benefit of the doubt—that is, everyone in our family except for Carter, who is a hard-headed truthteller.

What finally made me agree to let Isla and George go to Paris was remembering Al-Anon's instructions: "Don't play God" and "Let people make their decisions." I told her she could go, but she had to report back immediately if he began drinking. She agreed. I reassured myself that there would be other watchful adults around. as Isla's friend had also been accepted and would be there with her own family.

I went to Vernon, B.C., with Carter to spend time with my brother and his family. John was at summer school in Boston. I prayed George and Isla would have a wonderful time. One day at a time, I told myself.

From the outset of their trip, Isla and I were in constant communication, talking and texting. They arrived on a Friday morning and Isla sent pictures of them sightseeing, shopping, and adapting to the time change. They were having fun, she said. What she didn't tell me was that on Monday night, before her first day at ballet school, George came into her room and began rummaging through her bags, telling her he wanted to use her laptop, which she didn't bring. He then lost his balance and tumbled onto the floor. Clearly, he was drunk and looking for vodka bottles he'd stashed. When she asked if he'd been drinking, he became verbally abusive, behaving as he did with me. Isla was frightened but said nothing to me. She had learned to protect her father. "Yeah, yeah, everything's great!" she told me on the phone.

The next day, a Tuesday, George showed up with a black eye. Isla couldn't determine if it was from when he fell in her room or had to do with the broken oven door in their Airbnb.

Events took a more dangerous turn after Isla's first day of classes. George picked her up in a rented Audi convertible and, as they drove through Paris, Isla realized with mounting horror that her father was drunk. He was driving erratically. He headed the wrong way down a one-way street as cars honked madly at him, and they were still miles from their apartment near the Arc de Triomphe. Isla was terrified. George waved back at the honkers and laughed, oblivious to the chaos he was creating. "Isn't this fun, Isla?" he asked. "All these people honking at us; it's like we're in a video game." Thankfully, they returned to the Airbnb unharmed. But, even then, Isla said nothing to me. The second day, George showed up at the school in the same state and Isla drove with him again, terrified once more that he would crash.

While this was going on, there was another eruption. My sister Kathy was traveling to Paris, and had heard via our mother that George and Isla were there. She emailed George to say she'd like to see him while they were all there. Her message came out of the blue: neither George nor I had been in touch with her lately, as our relationship had gone through another bad spell.

George received her email after we had just hung up on what I thought was a reasonable conversation. He'd sounded tired, like he was possibly drinking, but I chalked it up to jet lag and a poor connection. Then I received a series of hostile texts: "Fuck you" and "Your sister is a cunt." There was way to deny that he was drinking again.

I immediately texted Isla to ask how she was. "I'm fine. Going out for dinner," she said, referring to a birthday dinner with her friend and her friend's family. They all, including George, went out and had a wonderful time. Afterward, George told the group to go and get gelato and that he was going back to the apartment to relax.

When Isla and her friend returned to the flat to spend the night before classes the next day, they found themselves locked out. Isla called me in desperation, not knowing what to do. I told her to wait. I told her I would call her friend's mother to ask her to pick them up and return them to her hotel so Isla could stay with them. The mother of Isla's friend immediately jumped into an Uber to get them.

I hung up, with a huge knot in my stomach, and began to look for flights to Paris. I called John in Boston, to see who could get there faster. We both booked red-eyes. All those sayings—"Who am I to play God?" and "One day at a time"—were of no use when the safety of the children was at stake.

Isla woke the next day intending to go to ballet school with her friend. That's what you do as the child growing up with addictive behaviour—you just get up and continue on with the day. It's normal to you. But Isla didn't have her dance gear, and was locked out of her Airbnb apartment.

Her friend's mother took the girls to the apartment and began pressing the buzzer from the street. No response. They were able to sneak in the front door as someone was leaving, and got into a tiny Parisian elevator, where they saw a key on the floor. It was the key to the apartment. How it ended up there remains a mystery. Isla had been texting her father that morning to say she needed to get into the flat for her dance gear. Had he thrown the key into the lift so she could retrieve her things? Had he taken two sets of keys in the night to buy more vodka and dropped one on his return? We still don't know.

But the girls weren't able to enter the apartment, even with the key. They could open the apartment door, but it was kept shut by a chain bolt inside. Isla texted me to say that she could see George through the crack in the door. He was sitting on the bed in the bedroom, dressed, wearing sunglasses, and using his iPad. He saw them and shouted, "What do you guys want?" Isla told him she needed her dance gear. She could see he was disoriented, and clearly hadn't slept. There were vodka bottles strewn all over and pill bottles by the bedside.

"You're drunk," she said.

"Fuck you," he responded.

"Did you attempt suicide?" she asked.

"I will do whatever the fuck I want, with no appreciation from all of you," he said, in front of her friend and her friend's mother.

Isla was madly texting me. I told her to call the emergency number. I knew that he was unfit and a potential harm to both Isla and himself, and that the state would have to deal with him.

Isla and her friend went downstairs and tried but couldn't connect with 112 (the equivalent of 911 in France). Fortunately, a kind woman witnessing the commotion helped them call an ambulance. When the medics arrived at the apartment, George came to the door nonchalantly, dressed like he had come home from a club. and let them in. He told them he wasn't suicidal.

I instructed Isla to keep telling the medics that George was a harm to himself and he was dangerous. I knew they would take that seriously coming from a minor. They took it seriously enough that George was taken to one hospital and assessed, then sent to Hôpital Maison Blanche, a psychiatric hospital near Père Lachaise Cemetery.

By then, John had arrived in Paris. I arrived that evening but the hospital would not let us see George until the next day, and it would be still longer before an English-speaking psychiatrist would be available. George showed no remorse. He wanted money, earplugs, his iPad (not allowed), and his book, Conrad Black's *Rise to Greatness: The History of Canada*. It was a book George had given to me the previous Christmas before telling me I'd never get through it because it was far above my intellectual level.

Back at the apartment, we went through George's things, which included 26-oz. vodka bottles and steroids. Isla found a bottle of Viagra and knew what it was for. Isla also logged on to George's iPad to see his conversations. There were many intimate chats with women he worked with in Arizona and Calgary, including a conversation with a woman he'd been in correspondence with for our entire marriage. She lived in Spain but was then in Paris, and they had planned to meet up when Isla was at ballet school.

Isla deleted all of the messages, trying to protect me. This is how sick families learn to operate. You're always investigating, monitoring, under the delusion that it offers control. You believe that if you can find out every little secret, you can control the situation. I was the same way with my mother.

George was hospitalized for five days. I picked him up when he was released, and then we went to get Isla from her class. I wanted to take the Metro, which is fast. George refused—he was above public transit—and insisted on a cab. As we traveled through Paris, I tried to keep the mood light by remarking on the architecture. He looked at me with hatred while imitating me. "You're being really mean," I told him. "You don't need to be mean; I know you don't want to be."

When we returned to the apartment, George showered, then demanded sex. "Please, I need this, it is the last time we will be together and it has been so long," he told me.

He wanted to hang on to our old patterning. I didn't.

"No, George."

"You don't love me anymore."

"I can't do this anymore. I've hit a wall."

It was the truth. I knew we had to separate. More importantly, I now knew that we would separate. I suggested giving it a year before re-evaluating, which is recommended in the 12-step world. They say not to make any drastic decisions within the first year of sobriety. Achieving one year of sobriety means it's more likely that another year of sobriety will follow. That's why there is such an emphasis on sobriety "birthdays." I laid out the terms.

"You're going to rehab and you're not going to live with us for one year to see if you can achieve abstinence," I told him. "You work on you and I'll work on me. We both need to be the best we can be for ourselves and for the children. That may be together or apart. Either way, we can still be supportive of each other's decisions. We have a year to figure this out."

It was a separation, but not necessarily divorce. "I know that we can have the best of each other," I told him optimistically. "But I also can understand how maybe it's time for a new chapter. Maybe I'm not the healthiest thing you can be around. But you keep working on you."

George spent the next month back in Sierra Tucson. When he went for the first time in 2015, he said he was there for PTSD caused by my affair and what I did to him. This time he admitted he had addiction issues and dove into the AA textbook.

Before he returned, he asked me to find him a nice place to live. Drawing a line, I said "no." When he returned, he moved into Le Germain.

It was a difficult period, and not only because of the separation. In September 2016. we learned that we did not qualify for a buyout of our flooded house on the Elbow River after all. George decided he would begin a renovation and move back in, with or without me. I was allowed to offer an opinion, but the message was clear: the Elbow River house was his house, and he was going to live there regardless of the state of his marriage.

As the new school year began, my focus was entirely on the children. I no longer believed in "Not me without you," and finally realized I could only be "me" without George. I was fatalistic about next steps, though—either George would figure himself out, or he wouldn't.

We kept our new arrangement under the radar. George didn't tell his closest friends we had split, but his story changed depending on who he was talking to. He told his family we were still working on the marriage. He told other friends and women he wanted to pursue that he was single.

Initially, I went along with keeping it private, just as I went along with George lying about where we married in Turkey. I saw it as "George's story," as though I was somehow not implicated. If people asked how Paris was, I told them it wasn't so great without going into detail. By November, however, I had reached a limit. "I am sick of pretending," I wrote in my journal.

George was facing his own challenges in his business life. He no longer had any pull with the Coyotes. His partners at AltaCorp were angry that he wasn't there showing leadership or drumming up new business.

In December, he stepped down from the board of AIMCo, the big provincial pension fund, which he regarded as one of his career highlights. He told me he was sad the kids didn't appreciate his professional accomplishments, and saw him simply as a "bad dad." He couldn't get over that he was considered a natural leader everywhere he went, except by his own family. In my journal, I noted a change in him: "When we married, George loved Calgary. He loved being a big fish in a little pond. Now he hates it."

We spent the holidays as a family: Christmas Eve with my parents and Christmas breakfast at George's sister's house. George spent much of the time stressing over arrangements and our relationship. I was the target of his frustration. I hadn't been sensitive and loving, he told me, and asked what I was doing toward getting us back together. "Your focus should be on you, your recovery and your goals," I told him.

At Christmas, I felt another rush of gratitude for my family. After Christmas, I began telling people we had separated. Technically, that was true. But there still were the dark hooks.

CHAPTER NINETEEN

Extremis

GEORGE AND I RANG IN New Year's 2017 separately, and being by myself allowed me to exhale and take stock. I could measure how much constant, heart-racing fear and anxiety I carried when I was around George. I saw how much energy I expended trying to tend to him and how controlling the relationship had been.

For George, the year began with another expedition, this time a trek to the South Pole with his close friend, Marshall. During the journey, Marshall became dehydrated to the point that he couldn't function. George pulled him for a day until they set up camp, something that must have taken tremendous strength for George, given that Marshall is much larger. After Marshall collapsed, they got socked in at camp because of weather. George still found time to call me on his satellite phone to berate me over what he perceived as my lack of love and support, and over me "fucking up" the marriage.

What made it different this time was that Marshall was in the tent with George and could hear all of George's verbal abuse, and George didn't seem to care. I assumed George was manic and delirious from exhaustion, but also from anxiety and self-reproach over not accomplishing his goal of reaching the South Pole. I could see now how he was trying to transfer that doubt and vulnerability to me.

When they returned, George made a show of sending a video from base camp to thank the family for our love and support. He was bearded and ruddy-skinned. He looked rough but seemed happy. He'd just had his first espresso in weeks, he told us.

In February, George took Isla to the Super Bowl in Houston. It may sound crazy after what happened in Paris, but both of them wanted to go. They both wanted another chance: George to prove he could be a responsible adult, and Isla to forgive her father and improve her relationship with him. Taking guidance from Al-Anon once again, I told myself I couldn't control everything and should stop trying, and I agreed. I thought the trip would be encouragement for George, who was honestly trying. It was also a chance for Isla to prove she could handle the responsibility of traveling with her difficult father. I sat her down and told her she had to communicate with me if, at any moment, she felt unsafe. She was not to hide her father's behaviour from me. She was a year older now, and a year smarter, and she'd learned by experience where denial could lead.

I feared he might try and buy her. That was George's modus operandi with me and, I would learn, other women, too: lavish shopping trips to Prada, Dolce & Gabbana, Versace. I thought about warning Isla but I didn't want to get between her and her father. I had to exercise self-control and let her make her own decisions about how she was going to handle herself and be around her dad. Isla in her adolescent wisdom figured things out on her own. When she returned, I asked her about the trip while driving her to school.

"What did you get?" I asked.

"Nothing," she said. "We went into Prada but I didn't let him buy anything."

They went to Christian Louboutin as well, but her response was the same.

I asked her why.

"Because, Mom, I didn't want him to think he could buy me."

I was pleased Isla could draw that line for herself. But I was also disgusted that George wanted to treat our daughter the way he treated me and countless other women.

That month I began watching *Big Little Lies*, the HBO series based on Liane Moriarty's best-selling novel. Set in an affluent community in

Monterey, California, a central plot line of the show revolves around the violent domestic abuse experienced by one character, played by Nicole Kidman. From the outside, everything in her life looks perfect: beautiful kids, attentive husband, a house out of *Architectural Digest*. In that community, too, appearances were everything.

As a rule, I avoided watching anything with violence. I tended to stick to comedies like *Modern Family* and *Schitt's Creek*, shows George ridiculed me for watching as he thought they marked me as uneducated and immature. Difficult as it was to watch the violence, however, I couldn't let go of *Big Little Lies*. It mirrored the reality of my hidden world so closely, the life I couldn't summon enough courage to change. It also did a great job of capturing the socialization of the privileged, the constant measuring of oneself against others, the rivalries stemming from the need to keep up with your neighbours. It perfectly captured the conflicts and insecurities that can exist between mothers in affluent circumstances: the way, for instance, Laura Dern's high-powered executive character feels alienated from the stay-at-home moms, and acts out her insecurities. Or how Reese Witherspoon's character flips between super-mom and super-bitch.

After George returned from the Super Bowl trip to Houston in February, he moved into the Elbow River house, even though it was still under renovation. Getting back together was not off the table, a fact I know many people won't understand. The plan was for him to go to therapy and we would make a decision after a year, and we were just over half way through. Things were up in the air.

One thing I felt strongly about was that I didn't want to return to that house. George had made it clear it was his territory, and he'd bought furniture without consulting me. I wasn't allowed to go inside without his express permission. There were cameras and alarms installed so that he would know who was there and, in particular, if I was there.

George was meanwhile living the high life as a single. He was taking steroids. His body looked pumped. He was driving a leased $140,000 BMW i8 he'd brought up illegally from Phoenix, and wearing Brunello Cucinelli everything. It was also clear he was involved with other women. My nanny described one woman as practically living there.

The South Pole excursion had not satiated him. Nothing was enough. Nothing brought lasting peace of mind. When he wasn't in Calgary, he was off on some exotic adventure, whether bone-fishing with U.S. Navy Seals off the coast of Molokai, or hunting for exotic big game in Africa—those trips where wealthy people in Range Rovers pay ridiculous sums of money to kill majestic endangered creatures. He sent Isla photographs of dead baby elephants and giraffes as a joke. A bad joke. I found the photos unsettling. He said he wanted to taxidermy a giraffe and display it in the house.

In July, Isla got her driver's license, which made her more independent. As a result, I spent many weekend nights alone, which was fine with me. It gave me more time to think about what I wanted and needed. I knew I had to address my marriage. People, including my family, were urging me to sit down with George, to come to a settlement and get on with my life.

The first thing any woman needs to be able to move on from a failed relationship is a sense of security. I felt that if I was to leave George, I would need to feel certain that I was safe and that the kids were safe. I would need no contact with him so I wouldn't get sucked back into our abusive dynamic. Similarly, I'd have to sure the children would not be used as tools of control. I would also need access to my community and some money.

As I carefully worked my way through these issues, I gained the courage to say out loud that I needed to make a final break with George. I drew a major line for myself on May 29, 2017, in my journal: "I will not be abused anymore." Not physically or verbally. I understood and was willing to say that I had experienced abuse. I began to find my voice. At a family dinner with George's parents, his father kept interrupting me. In the past, it would have shut me down. Instead, I respectfully countered, "If you could please let me finish, I'll explain."

Meanwhile, it was the usual up and down with George. He took John and Carter to Hawaii that summer, an attempt to reconnect with the boys while he was living healthier, or at least not drinking. The boys reported George seemed calmer, less manic, and that he had indeed stopped drinking. I was in touch with him regularly, acceding to his demands for check-ins, morning and night. I was a bit more assertive, telling him what I wanted full financial disclosure. Of course, that only made him angry and brought on more insults.

In September, George and I met on the patio of Cucina, a popular bistro restaurant near his office, for lunch. He was training to get back to Everest. "You're not showing me commitment," he said. Again, it was my problem.

"I'm getting mixed messages," I told him, mentioning the woman he was known to be involved with and the fact he had been seen with others. I raised her name specifically to make him flinch, to watch his reaction.

"Oh my God, whatever, Karen," he said. "There's no one concrete. It's all bullshit."

I needed to see him tell lie after lie without flinching. He was a pro. As we walked from the patio through the restaurant, George grabbed me and kissed me on the lips, suddenly affectionate after our difficult conversation. I found it odd.

"Bye," I said, and left, assuming that he was returning to his office.

As I was walking away, my gut told me to return to the restaurant. I did, and saw George sitting at a table with the woman I'd mentioned earlier, the one he said he wasn't involved with.

I looked him in the eye and watched him get flustered.

A woman who worked in the restaurant came up to me.

"Can I help you?"

"No."

I knew what I had to do.

CHAPTER TWENTY

The End

AN HOUR LATER, George called, panicked, trying to manage the situation. "Oh my God, Karen, can you believe it? That's pretty funny."

I didn't laugh. "Yeah, I can believe it, George."

I felt the power dynamic between us flip. I remained calm, but George was scrambling. He suggested we see a new movie about Vincent Van Gogh. I agreed to keep things civil. We went to the movie, the last date we'd have.

I called up the lawyer I'd consulted years earlier. I sat down with Isla to tell her I was going to ask her father for a divorce. I added that I thought maybe I'd wait until after Christmas so everyone could have a good Christmas. Isla stared at me in amazement. "Why would you do that?" she asked. "We haven't had a good Christmas ever."

She was right. Christmas in the Gosbee house was filled with lavish gifts, the latest Apple products, and designer clothing, but it was all about quantity—not about love. I would tell George I'd purchased presents for the kids and the family, and he'd go out and buy more. He would then invariably express anger that my gifts to him hadn't involved enough thought. And then, of course, there was the Christmas Day suicide attempt. Isla was the sensible one. "Mom, give your head a shake."

I also told Isla I'd been asked out by a man I'd known for years, although not well. I was thinking of saying yes. What did she think? She encouraged me. George was away on a climbing trip at the time, but I knew the minute

I appeared in public with someone else, it would get back to him, and that there would be consequences.

I went out to brunch with this man. Our second date was a fund-raiser where we ended up seated at a table that was broadcast on the big Jumbotron screen capturing the event. *George is going to find out about this for sure*, I thought nervously. It did get back to him that I'd gone out, but fortunately he misidentified my date as someone else entirely.

Even before I mentioned divorce to George, he would regularly text to tell me he was going to hire the best lawyer available and destroy me. "Legal abuse" is another common component of affluent intimate-partner violence. Here, the legal system itself becomes a weapon—the "I'm going to ruin you" threat, whether financial or otherwise. In any separation or divorce fight, the affluent abuser has the resources to sustain an aggressive court battle. He (or she) can drag the partner repeatedly to court over frivolous issues to deplete her financial resources, or create a conflict of interest with the most reputable law firms in town so that the partner cannot get effective representation. Under our current legal system, there's no way to stop this behaviour.

I didn't know our financial picture, but I did know that, so long as George was feeling poor, he was less likely to deliver on his occasional threats to hire the best lawyer in the country to completely destroy me and take the kids away and make them hate me. The threats made me sick, but those feelings were offset somewhat by George's fear that, if we both hired lawyers and proceeded to a round of legal discovery, he would have to disclose his true financial situation. He would do anything to avoid that.

He also feared losing me, some of the time. "Miserable with you," he would text. "Miserable without you. DON'T WANT TO LIVE." Or, "Thanks 4 being the best friend anyone could ever have. Thx 4 always believing in me and especially 4 being patient and waiting for me I owed u so much." In the next breath, he would be belligerent: "I'm coming home to file for a divorce." Or, "I would suggest you contact a lawyer this week." After he found out I was dating, he threatened me directly: "I don't want this to end violently," one text read. "And when I get home I will be at an all-time depression and scared of what I will do and people I will hurt."

A text that seemed to refer to Argentina was particularly frightening: "First time I have been this manic in five years and that didn't end well."

By then, I couldn't pretend any more. "I am fucking terrified of him," I wrote in my journal. I told a police officer who also attended Al-Anon that I was planning to ask George for a divorce. After I described George's history, he laid out the risks in a matter-of-fact way. "He's threatening suicide, so he's one step away from being homicidal," he said. He gave me a list of instructions: get a second phone to make sure you can contact your kids. Change the locks on the house. Install a second door that opens outwards because it's harder to kick two doors in.

Then he said something that chilled me. He told me that, if George tried to get into the house and I needed to call 911, I should say a stranger is trying to break in. "Don't say it's your husband," he said. Police rank domestic disputes lower in terms of priority, he explained. A stranger is treated as the greater threat, contrary to the fact most people are harmed or killed by people they know.

Amid all the threats, George's assistant called to tell me George wanted to go to marriage counselling. At the time, she was also condo shopping for the woman George said he wasn't seeing.

We decided to have a counselling appointment on Wednesday, November 8. I decided to use the appointment as a neutral space to tell George I wanted a divorce. I didn't want to do it when we were alone because I didn't feel safe. I knew that the most dangerous time for a woman in an abusive relationship is when she announces she's leaving. That's when the abusive partner often tries to seize control, often with violence, because he knows he's losing his grip. I was scared of George and didn't trust him. The truth, too, was that I also didn't fully trust myself either. I had a pattern of backing down.

I followed the police officer's instructions. I bought a new phone, and then asked the sales clerk for help logging on because the password on my Shaw account had been changed on me. I needed to set up my emails to be downloaded to the second phone. The clerk in the store explained they couldn't do it because the account wasn't in my name, but I managed to pull some empathy out of her. She could sense I was in a vulnerable position. She let me change the password so I could access my email again.

While this drama was happening, I noticed an older man in the shop watching me. He finally approached. "You look really familiar to me," he said, explaining he was buying a laptop with his wife. It turns out he was the general manager at the Hudson's Bay department store when I had worked there as a teenager: "You haven't changed at all," he said. It was a surreal moment.

Working retail again was always one of my backup plans for after I left George. I knew I could at least do that. I told myself that I could walk away from him and have nothing. The day before the appointment, I had the locks changed on the Aspen house. The locksmith came late in the afternoon and told me he couldn't do it that day: he didn't have the proper parts. I was in a panicked state and started crying. He took pity on me, or suddenly understood the gravity of the situation, and drove across town to pick up the needed part. I will forever be indebted to that man for his kindness.

By then I had written out and rehearsed what I would say to George many times over. There had been too many times when we'd be having a good conversation and then things would suddenly flip and he'd attack. My mind would always go blank and I wouldn't know how to respond. I could barely manage a "fuck you!"—the lowest denominator in communication.

We had gone together as a couple to this marriage counsellor a few times, and a few times each of us on our own as well. As usual, George had difficulty committing to the process. He cancelled a lot, but we both liked the counsellor, an older fellow, a cancer survivor and widower.

On this occasion, we arrived separately at his suburban home. We met in the room he kept for his practice, which had two leather easy chairs, running water, and crystals. The counsellor kicked things off. The last time we had met, he had been encouraging me to articulate my feelings, and he began now by asking me to be communicative. *Well,* I thought. *Here goes.*

I stumbled over what I wanted to say, despite having rehearsed it a million times, but I did manage to express that I had grown tremendously over the past year and that I could no longer exist within the terms of our relationship. I was crystal clear that I wanted a divorce; I'd finally come to understand that there would be no "me" as long as I was with him. When

I finished, not ten minutes into the session, George stood up and walked out. He didn't say a word. The therapist didn't know how to respond, but asked me how I was feeling. I was shaking. My heart was racing. I left the room, too, and got into my car.

As I was driving away, George called. He wanted to talk and asked me to pull over and get into his car. I refused. I told him to come and sit in my car. Still, I was terrified.

He said he wanted another chance. He said that his experiences over the past few years had made him realize his undying love for me. "I love you," he said. "We can do this." He admitted he hadn't been straight with me. He revealed he'd had an affair in Phoenix with a younger woman who'd reminded him of me. He said he loved her and considered leaving the family to begin a family with her. "I couldn't do it because I loved our family so much," he said.

I spoke as calmly as I could. "Let me think about it," I told him, adding, once again, that I needed financial disclosure. "Whatever decision I make, George, I need to see the financials and I need to see them now. I've been asking for this for the entire marriage, especially since 2014. You're not showing me everything, and the only way I will get it now is through discovery."

I left the conversation realizing that George had believed that he could suck me back into the relationship with his confession, as though he were finally coming clean. I was also convinced that his lack of money was the primary thing that was keeping him in the relationship. If he'd been feeling flush, he would have left years ago.

I felt unsafe as I returned home, and decided to go to my parents' house in Canmore, outside the city, since they were away. John was at school in Boston, and Isla and Carter were happy to stay with friends for a couple of nights. I didn't let on how scared I was.

The next few days were filled with the usual up-and-down text messaging. "We can do this. I need you. We are meant to be" was followed by "You fckn cunt I will destroy you and bring you down. Your name is trash around town. I am hiring the best lawyer."

Then, on the Friday night after I'd asked for a divorce, George began serial texting, a dead giveaway that he was drinking. We went six hours going over the same ground, like we were on a hamster wheel. He kept pleading with me to meet with him at the Elbow River house so he could show me papers explaining our finances. Every fiber in my body told me that would be a mistake, and I managed to listen to my instincts. It came out that George was in a panic about the details of the Coyotes deal. He didn't want it exposed that he was not the majority shareholder in Gozco, and that all of his grandstanding as the team's "owner" in Arizona had been a sham.

George's assistant, who of course was paid by him and generally loyal to him, also warned me not to go to the Elbow River house alone. She'd seen how angry he was. She'd heard him say "I'm going to take her down." She heard the hatred in his voice.

Finally, on that Friday night, I told George I needed to sleep and that I'd be turning my phone off. I woke to a string of abusive texts that ended around 3 a.m. Then, nothing. When I didn't hear from him on Saturday, I thought it was odd and out of character for him but he had said he might go rock climbing or shooting with friends. When there was no contact by Sunday morning, I began to panic. I knew it would be impossible for George to remain silent from 3 a.m. on Saturday morning right through until Sunday. He'd never gone that long before in our marriage without contacting me. The kids were worried, too. Isla, studying for a social studies midterm, couldn't focus because George wasn't responding to her texts. Usually, he replied within seconds. His assistant was also frantic. George's texts to her had also stopped at 3 a.m. Saturday.

We began making calls. The first was to the friend he'd said he was going shooting with, then to the mountain guide he used for climbing, then to George's parents. We found out he'd cancelled a shooting trip on Friday night. We heard from the climbing friend that George wasn't with him, either. Nobody had seen or heard from him. By Sunday night, I had a sickening sense of dread, and a certitude about what had happened. I knew I had to drive to the house.

Coincidently, my brother Scott called as I was leaving. When I told him where I was going, he made me swing by and pick him up. He wanted to be there in case there was a confrontation. I didn't say anything to him, but

I knew in my heart there would be no confrontation. I knew that George was dead. I knew where he was and how he had done it. When I'd gone out on a date, he'd threatened to hang himself.

By the time Scott and I arrived at the house, the sun was setting. The front gate was locked, so I circled around to use the back door. As I approached, I could see George's silhouette through the glass window. He was hanging from the railing of the second-floor balcony.

My mind was stuttering. *He did it. He did it. He did it.* After all the threats and attempts, he'd finally done it. I was numb as Scott followed me into the house. I started telling myself to hold it together—*You're okay, Karen; you can do this*— the same mantra that got me through so many difficult moments in childhood. Behind me, I could hear Scott calling 911, but the words sounded like static.

Scott is a doctor. He took one look at George and knew there was no need for urgency or an ambulance.

I walked toward George. After years and years of worrying about this moment, girding myself for this moment, I was not ready for it. You can never be ready for it. My mind ran back over the past several days. The meeting with the therapist, our last conversations, my fears, the maniacal texting, and then the silence. I went upstairs to see what George had seen. I looked around the house. There was nothing there: no suicide note, which surprised me; no signs of a disturbance; no papers of the kind George was promising to show me.

Soon I heard another voice—George's younger sister, Jean, wailing with grief downstairs. George's parents, also worried by his silence, had sent her to check on the situation.

The police arrived and an officer wanted to question me. I looked down to my flashing phone. My kids were calling. They knew their father was dead. Scott had called our parents after he dialed 911, and they immediately reached out to Isla and Carter, not knowing that I hadn't told them. I wanted to be heading toward them before calling them. They would need me for this nightmare.

I quickly called John in Boston. He booked the first flight home. I ask the officer if I could leave to be with my children. He looked at me with concern. "Are you sure you can drive?" he asked. How could he know I'd been hardwired since childhood to soldier through crises? I was thinking to myself, "Why wouldn't I be okay?"

Scott, thankfully, offered to stay and deal with everything. I hugged him and left, driving toward Isla. It was almost dark and I drove robotically, understanding along the way why the officer asked me if I was okay to drive. I barely noticed a thing on the road.

Memories flashed in my head. George and I getting married in Turkey, so young and unprepared. The early fights. Me with my babies alone in big, beautiful houses. George drunk, asleep at the dinner table. George curled in a fetal position. George threatening suicide. George threatening me. I saw those looks of his that terrified me and kept me walking on eggshells. I thought of us fighting, laughing, fighting, then having sex. I thought of the facade we constructed.

Then I thought of George's fist pounding my face in a Buenos Aires hotel room, and me calling the police after George pinned me down on the bathroom floor and tried to strangle me, and my daughter not understanding why I had called the police—George hadn't actually hurt me. That astonishing moment—Isla's response—I remembered more clearly than anything.

I wanted to believe George was finally in a place of love and peace. He'd spent so much of his forty-eight years on earth fighting: fighting for success, fighting for social approval, fighting his addictions, fighting me, fighting to stay alive. Now that fight was over. But it would be a lie to say I wasn't angry at him.

Fucking George, fucking George, fucking George, I thought. *You did it. You did it.*

CHAPTER TWENTY-ONE

Aftermath

WHEN I GOT TO THE HOUSE, I clung to Isla and Carter. The house quickly filled with people, including many of the kids' friends, some of whom I didn't know. I was torn, wanting to tell everyone that we needed our space, but one of Isla's friends had a father who had attempted suicide and I didn't want her to feel alienated. George's father called. "We love you," he said. "We know you did everything you could to keep him alive. We don't blame you."

My journal entries that night were filled with emotion, confusion, shock. "The sadness one feels with that choice. Or is it even a choice?" I wrote. "The violence he inflicted on himself. The turmoil within. He was so tortured. George all alone, dead. Dead to the world. Gone. It all seems so overwhelming. George spun magic whenever he was excited about something. When he let his light shine he was a beautiful person. Unfortunately, he could not figure out how to let it shine in a stable fashion."

"He did it," I wrote. "He had tried so many times. . . . Unimaginable that he actually succeeded."

It wasn't until a few days later that I cried for the first time, alone in the car. To be brutally honest, I don't know if I was crying because I was terrified of what was to come or if I was feeling sorry for myself. My sadness wasn't about George's death. The fact that George died as he did, unable to find help, was an unthinkable tragedy. But as someone who had watched him struggle as he did, George's death came as a relief. His struggles to stay alive wore on everyone, not least himself.

George's funeral was the following Saturday, and the intervening week was a blur. The news spread quickly in the Elbow Park neighbourhood after someone saw emergency vehicles at the house. As it happened, Peters & Co., where George worked in the 1990s, was hosting a mental health symposium on the Monday. It ended up focusing on his suicide. I received a flood of calls from George's former colleagues afterward.

Some people close to George were floored. Others told me they knew he was struggling. Others didn't acknowledge his death at all, which made me realize that we still don't know how to talk about suicide. Some newspapers used the euphemism "died suddenly" to refer to his death.

One woman who knew both George and me approached me at the dog park a few days later. I was prepared for her to express condolences. "Is that your dog?" she asked, with no mention of George. "Yes," I answered. That was the end of our conversation.

There were more surreal moments. Our neighbour, Allan Markin, a former CEO of Canadian Natural Resources Limited and a co-owner of the Calgary Flames hockey team, offered to donate $100,000 to the Hotchkiss/Mathison Centre for Mental Health Research & Education if I donated George's brain for study. We scrambled to figure out how to do it because we supported the Hotchkiss Brain Institute, which focuses on adult neuroscience. In the end, we were told that research couldn't be conducted on a brain that had been deprived of oxygen for so long. Al, one of the most philanthropic men in Calgary, still donated the money, for which I am most grateful.

Throughout that week, the children and I remained in close contact with George's parents. The funeral was to be held at their church, St. Stephen's Anglican, and be officiated by their minister, Brian Pearson. I told them it was our wish that we be candid about George's mental illness at the funeral. I explained that John wanted to speak and that I would say something at the reception.

They were concerned and wanted to see what John would write. When we met with Brian Pearson, he read John's eulogy and said he was moved by it.

The huge turnout on Saturday was a tribute to the number of people and communities that George touched. So many people showed up that the church couldn't accommodate everyone. As our family walked in together, John tried to lighten the mood. "You know Dad would have wanted us all to get spray tans to honor him," he whispered.

Brian's homily was beautiful. It addressed the need for society to speak openly about mental illness:

> *Human communities that are capable of producing not only heroic people, but also healthy people, such communities welcome the whole person— listening not just to the bravado, but also to the brokenness. They permit not only "I can do this!" but also "I'm scared shitless.*
>
> *Mental illness in the modern day is no different than it was in any other day. It can hide behind the brightest smile, behind the noblest of intentions, like a long shadow extending out from behind a tall statue—the brighter the light, the darker the shadow.*
>
> *But mental illness can also be coaxed out into the light of day by safe communities where we say, it's okay to feel broken. It's okay to feel weak. It's okay to feel frightened. It's okay, in other words, to be human.*
>
> *And if it is okay to be human, knowing we all hear troubling voices calling to us from the shadows, then we can encourage each other to love ourselves, even those shadowy places with the dark voices.*
>
> *We love ourselves into wholeness. Not just the sunny parts of ourselves, but the dark parts too, especially the dark parts. They are the parts that require the most love, and attention, and care.*

John titled his eulogy "The Kaleidoscope," based on a toy George had bought him from a business trip. I felt great pride watching him speak. He was devastated by George's death, as were Isla and Carter. In his tribute, John emphasized how his father was ill, and how he had sought help for his illness, and how that help wasn't enough: "We are here today because everything he did to try to defeat his illnesses, and he tried a lot to overcome them, did not work. In wake of this, there lies an opportunity for us to improve the dialogue surrounding mental health diseases.

Let us seek to eliminate the shame and the social stigma around these matters."

The reception was held at a golf and country club. Jean, his sister, wanted a big celebratory party, with a sound system, drinks, the works. It's what George would have wanted, she said. My instinct was to scale it back and I didn't want alcohol, but she was probably right about what George would have wanted.

At the reception, a number of people close to George spoke, including his friend Marshall from the South Pole expedition, George's lawyer, and his cousins. I read a poem from Marianne Williamson entitled "Our Deepest Fear." George liked it, and I would send it to him when he would threaten that he couldn't go on and didn't want to live:

> *Our deepest fear is not that we are inadequate.*
> *Our deepest fear is that we are powerful beyond measure.*
> *It is our light, not our darkness*
> *that most frightens us.*
>
> *We ask ourselves,*
> *Who am I to be brilliant, gorgeous, talented, fabulous?*
> *Actually, who are you not to be?*
> *You are a child of God.*
>
> *Your playing small*
> *Does not serve the world.*

One of George's friends came to the funeral with a photographic memorial of George that showed off the exotic animals they had shot in Africa, including a baby elephant and a giraffe.

After the funeral, John and I read the suicide notes Scott found the night we went to the house. George had left them on a high fireplace mantle, where I hadn't seen them when I'd first looked around in my shocked state. The police read them first, then released them to Scott. There was one for George's parents, one for me, one for the children, notes for some of his business partners, and one for his assistant—even one for one of our dogs.

Reading them, it was clear George had been drinking when he wrote them, and that my fear of meeting him alone had been justified. In his note to the children, he blamed himself for his behaviour. His note to me boiled with anger: "You did this to me, I hate you," it read in part. After John read the note to me, he stood up, walked to the kitchen sink and burned it. It was a reflexive reaction, and a healthy one: we didn't want to forget George, but we didn't want any reminder of hatred.

But the reality is that the hatred is seared into our collective family memory. Even now, the kids sometimes refer to "the look," that piercing glare of hatred George gave me across the dinner table.

CHAPTER TWENTY-TWO

No More Secrets

NEWS OF GEORGE'S SUICIDE was met with disbelief in Calgary and far beyond. He was only forty-eight and appeared to have everything to live for: three beautiful children, international success, wealth, political and social influence. Media coverage highlighted his accomplishments, such as how he'd built two investment companies from the ground and been a co-owner of the Arizona Coyotes' NHL hockey team. He played an active role in national public policy, as well, having served prime ministers Stephen Harper and Justin Trudeau.

The tributes mentioned George's keen intelligence, his natural curiosity, his boundless enthusiasm, and his tireless fundraising for charities. He wasn't just a business guy. His long list of hobbies included hunting, mountain-climbing, heli-skiing, reading, yoga, and cooking. The *Calgary Herald* called him a "gifted, visionary leader." *The Globe and Mail* in Toronto referred to him as a "Calgary titan."

George's friend Brett Wilson, the investor and television star, expressed his shock on Twitter: "Another dead by one's own hand. Another dark cloud that wasn't seen by family and friends."

That's how it looked from the outside: Instagram perfect. And there was truth in it. To look at photos of George and me smiling at black-tie charity events or with our children on family holidays in China, Italy, France, and the Caribbean, you'd never guess our marriage and our family was in crisis. You'd never guess I was living in fear for my life. But our family lived with that "dark cloud" for decades and the roller-coaster of George's alcohol and substance misuse, his suicide attempts, his violence, and his repeated attempts to get better. He'd been diagnosed with ADD, bi-polar disorder, and borderline personality disorder, and prescribed a long list of medications that he either didn't take or took sporadically, fearing they'd dull what it was that made him successful and brought him accolades.

How things looked was everything to George. Again, perception was everything. He associated personal success with public approbation and external recognition. He didn't feel any personal satisfaction without it. He believed his reputation would be destroyed if his mental illness, or his behaviours, were revealed. That terrified him more than any mortal threat to his health could have done.

The irony is that George's death revealed the life he kept well hidden. Untangling his estate was a shocking wake-up call, one that forced me to see how little I knew about our financial affairs. We'd written wills in 2004 and updated them in 2008, but George hadn't renewed his life insurance, which I didn't know about. I hired an estate lawyer, who began the complex task of connecting the dots between George's companies and assets. We found accounts that had been in overdraft for years.

George's manic behaviour in his final years was spelled out in monthly Amex bills averaging $60,000 to $80,000. The money went to global expeditions: a trip to the South Pole, $85,000; big-game hunting, $60,000; the climbing portion of a trip to Mt. Carstenaz in Papua, New Guinea, $34,000. He spent $11,000 on a dirt bike he bought in Arizona and used once. The amount he spent staying at Le Germain would have paid a teacher for a year. When we went through his closets, there were a lot of suits that still had price tags on them. All to create that veneer of affluence that he needed and wanted the world to see.

I also learned just how much financial pressure George had been under. He was facing a call note on a big loan that was about to come due on November 13, the day after his body was found. He had been pinning his hopes on an investment that could bring in millions but hadn't delivered anything yet.

The bank called me in late November, wanting a meeting. There, I received another shock, one that destabilized me completely: I learned that George had transferred a huge sum from a business account to a personal account and then burned through it. The papers I had been forced to co-sign included a collateral mortgage on the house, and increases to the personal line of credit that supported George's large lifestyle in Phoenix. I was terrified that I would be on the hook to repay a massive debt I didn't even know about, money that I didn't have. Yet another nightmare.

I needed a lawyer. A very good lawyer. I retained Bob Thompson, a Calgary attorney who came highly recommended. I will forever be indebted to Bob for ably guiding me through the difficult and intimidating days and months that followed.

The lockbox app on George's phone unearthed more secrets: photographs, many of naked and semi-naked women, taken in Arizona and at the Sochi Olympics. Often they would be wearing Christian Louboutin shoes and white buttoned shirts, as he had liked to dress me. One of the subjects was the woman from Spain with whom he had intended to meet up with in Paris. There were also pictures of a woman who lived in Calgary who charged a flight to George's credit card after his death. His texts revealed many explicit interactions with these women, including a set with a woman who'd been a childhood friend of mine.

There was more. I learned one of George's affairs had included a woman who had worked in private accounts at our bank. She confessed to me and apologized. It was in an August 2018 cover story about George in the *Globe and Mail's Report on Business* magazine, "Death of a Calgary Titan: The Spectacular Rise and Tragic Fall of George Gosbee," that we learned that George had met up with a woman he was seeing during the trip to India that he took with John in 2015. That story described George as "a man who could be hostile and vindictive to anyone who questioned how he ran his businesses." What no one knew—how could they know?—is that he was also that way to anyone who questioned how he ran his home.

I found a notebook from George's time at the Hoffman Process in 2012, which underscored how terrified he was as being found out as a person with mental health issues, of being seen as "weak." He wrote about killing himself, saying it would be easier for him to do if his parents weren't alive, and how it would be devastating to the kids. "But I don't want to die," he wrote. "I'm trapped."

In a short diary dating back to the 1990s, George expressed his beliefs about mental illness in the investment industry. "I'm convinced the investment business attracts only manic depressives," he wrote in 1998. "For seasoned portfolio managers," he added, "their moods fluctuate with the cycles in their portfolio." He questioned how they stayed in business, or even stayed alive.

Another entry talked about how he feared being "ruined in the community" if his addictions and behaviours were known. The sad part is that he was correct. His "community" would have been judgmental, not empathetic.

The revelations kept coming throughout the year after George's death. I found his gun registration, which allowed him to carry unrestricted and restricted firearms, including handguns. He'd lied on the form to obtain it. One question: "During the past five (5) years, have you threatened or attempted suicide, or have you suffered from or been diagnosed or treated by a medical practitioner for: depression; alcohol, drug or substance misuse; behavioural problems; or emotional problems?" George should have answered "yes" to all that, and also to this question: "During the past five (5) years, do you know if you have been reported to the police or social services for violence, threatened or attempted violence, or other conflict in your home or elsewhere?" He didn't.

There was one particular piece of paper I came across that shook me the most. It was a letter to George dated a few months before his death, from the concierge of the Buenos Aires hotel where George had beaten me in 2012. It confirmed that George had gone back and stayed there again. I was shocked. How could he have returned? I would never have been able to go back, out of shame, knowing that I'd trashed my room there. More to the point, how could he have returned given his memory of what happened between us?

Some of the surprises were out of left field. Isla was contacted by 23 and Me, the company behind the DNA testing kit. A few years earlier, George had gotten both John and Isla to take DNA tests because he wanted to check out the technology for a prospective business venture. The company told Isla they had found a match with a relative. We then learned that George had an older brother: his parents had given him up for adoption, something his parents never told anyone about. This man was named John. He had been named Gerald by George's parents, but his adopted family had preferred John—a strange coincidence, because the Gosbee family had a tradition going back generations of naming the firstborn boy John. I could never understand why George, the firstborn, wasn't named John. (Everyone had told us to start the tradition again when our John was born, which we did.)

I took over talking to George's brother until he contacted George's mother, who needed time to absorb the news. She forbade me and Isla to tell anyone. As it happened, Isla quite innocently told others she had a new uncle, so there was friction with her grandmother. I explained to Isla that she could honor her grandmother without perpetuating secrecy: "You love her and support her, and also say that you have talked to this man and he's going to be in your life."

On the first anniversary of George's death, November 11, 2018, our family honored his life in our own way. We spent the night at home, eating George's favourite foods: pizza, chips, wine gums, KFC with fries and gravy, and beef tenderloin with no veggies, accompanied by Diet Coke, wine, and Scotch. We reminisced with funny stories that celebrated George's idiosyncrasies and all of the things we cherished about him, including his ability to be a playful adult-child, something he began to lose in 2008.

Publicly, George's legacy has been enshrined in various ways--there's a scholarship in his name at the Haskayne School of Business at the University of Calgary. Ten thousand trees were planted in his honor on Father's Day 2018 at a local conservation site where he sat on the board. I was invited but declined. I thanked George's friend, who organized the event, but chose to spend the day with my own father. Our family has founded the Gosbee Family Foundation, which received charitable status in April 2019. We want to provide information and access to mental health services as well as referral services to anyone experiencing mental health illness or challenged by the initial stages of mental illness.

Finding Meaning

AS WE SORTED THROUGH the estate, George's publicist called to tell me that media wanted to interview me about George's illness and suicide, and its effects on the family. I agreed without hesitation. I wanted others to learn from our experiences. I also wanted to try to help eradicate the internal and societal shame and stigma that surround addiction, depression, and mental illness. I didn't mention in these interviews the violence I experienced. I wasn't ready to speak about it, and frankly I didn't know if I ever would be.

The response I received was overwhelming. Some people said they sensed George wasn't well. Others shared their own mental health issues or suicidal thoughts and experiences. After one luncheon I spoke at, a man who was a good business friend of George's approached me to admit that he initially thought that I had no right to "defame" George and talk about his mental health challenges. Now he understood why I was doing it, he said.

Not everyone was so understanding. George's parents and family were uncomfortable with my decision to speak up. Other friends and associates of George didn't want his legacy and, indirectly, their own reputations associated with mental illness or addiction. Even though I begin any public mention of George by expressing my gratitude for all that he gave me, for our children, and also what he taught me about humanity, they felt my openness eclipsed, even tainted, George's accomplishments, a view that I believe is part of the problem.

The fact George accomplished as much as he did while struggling as he did is amazing, but his life is also an example of systemic and societal failures to address mental illness. Our relentless focus on and celebration of "success" makes it still more difficult for people to seek help for illnesses wrongly stigmatized.

I also heard, after coming forward, that some people were saying I was the reason George killed himself. A few were angry that I didn't mention my affair in interviews, which I felt was unfair. I hadn't mentioned George's serial affairs, either, but I was frank about the troubles in our relationship. My cousin bumped into a man from Calgary when she was on vacation in Mexico who told her the reason George could never get healthy was because of "what Karen did to him." Blaming one person is easy. It also sidesteps dealing with the complexity of mental illness.

I suppose I should have expected this but an Al-Anon representative got in touch with me to ask me not to mention the organization by name. I explained that I'd never betray anyone's identity, but that I wanted to speak about Al-Anon because Al-Anon had saved me. More people should be aware of it as a resource, I said: "I have a hard time with your tradition of secrecy. It needs to be updated. People have to be able to talk." Ironically, one of Al-Anon's slogans is: "You are only as sick as your secrets."

Still other people warned me not to mention that George's suicide took place in our house. "You'll affect the property value," they said, as if it were occupied by ghosts or an evil spirit. It's the same sort of superstitious belief evident when people talk about people with mentally illness having "demons." But every house contains a history of both joy and tragedy, and often even death. We need to eradicate such thinking and focus on helping people who are struggling.

We will never be able to address mental illness or suicide or domestic violence without being able to look at it and speak of it clearly.

Let's face facts. More than 4,000 Canadians and 48,000 Americans die of suicide every year. Middle-aged men are overwhelmingly the most likely to kill themselves, and usually over money problems. Women are far more likely be diagnosed with depression, but men are three times more likely to kill themselves.

Success and wealth offer no protection, as we saw with the deaths of Robin Williams, Anthony Bourdain, and designer Kate Spade. In my family, neither our wealth, which could buy the "best" private rehabs and therapists, nor our medical connections could save George. My father and my brother are both neurologists. George's father was also a physician.

We need to talk more about suicide, and that means not dictating how people, particularly people who have attempted suicide or who ideate about suicide, talk about it. That's an important point made by Jess Stohlmann-Rainey in her 2019 essay "How 'Safe Messaging' Gaslights Suicidal People." Jess, a suicide attempt survivor, writes about how suicidal people are stigmatized for talking about their experiences in ways that don't conform to "strategic, safe and positive" suicidal messaging. The worry is that sharing details about suicide will result in copycats or suicide "clusters," even though there isn't an academic consensus on that theory.

Jess noticed how public pressure caused Netflix to edit out a central, graphic suicide scene in its controversial series *13 Reasons Why*, about a suicide in a high school. Yet they didn't edit out all of the rape, violence, and bullying that lead up to it, she points out: "Suicide being the result of a series of traumas is what gets edited out, not the trauma itself." And this doesn't help suicidal people.

Suicide is always constructed as a "pathology," Jess continues, which means that it's something inside her that needs to be "ferreted out and removed," which means that a suicidal person can never be trusted. That kind of attitude creates even greater distress for her, Jess writes: "It made me vulnerable, fragile, needing protection and oversight." When she was feeling suicidal, she found content about suicide soothing: "It allowed me to work out some of the suicidal energy that vibrated through my bones." Learning about people who thought about, or even died from suicide, made her feel less alone. "All of us deserve the dignity of owning and sharing our stories without mediation or infiltration by systemic silence and shame," she says. I agree.

We see similar secrecy and shame around domestic violence, which is still treated as something that's private, and not other people's business. The violence in my marriage began days after our 1994 wedding and escalated. I'm not alone. In 2019, after a series of horrifying cases, the Calgary Police

Service referred to the rising incidence of domestic violence and domestic homicide in my city as an "epidemic" (it's even worse now as of writing, thanks to the COVID-19 pandemic). A 2016 study revealed more than 750,000 Canadians had experienced spousal conflict, abuse, or violence in the previous five years. That same year, some 93,000 cases of domestic violence were laid with police and that's the tip of the iceberg—we know more than eighty percent of cases are not reported.

In the U.S., the Centers for Disease Control estimate that one on four women will experience intimate partner violence at some point in her lifetime. At least five million acts of domestic violence occur annually to women over the age of eighteen, including 1.5 million physical assaults and rapes. The World Health Organization has called "domestic violence," specifically domestic homicide, a "global epidemic." According to a 2018 United Nations report, the home is the most dangerous place for a woman.

There's more. A 2019 study from the University of Guelph determined that a woman or girl is killed, on average, every 2.5 days in Canada. While the homicide rate is higher for men, women are killed far more frequently by an intimate partner or relative (two-thirds of cases).[8]

I saw a need to discuss this data and the ways mental illness, addiction, violence, and family trauma intersect, and how they affect the entire family, creating trauma and patterns we are destined to repeat through the generations if they are not addressed. This is something I know first-hand, having been raised in a family where there was substance misuse, depression, and an attempted suicide. Then I married into it. I'm not unique.

The years I spent in and out of health facilities and various programs with George gave me insight how the family is overlooked in the larger picture. Children are also victims, directly and indirectly. We know that children who grow up in violent or abusive homes suffer trauma, which

---

8　See the report *#CallitFemicide: Understanding Gender-Related Killings of Women and Girls in Canada 2018*, published by the Canadian Femicide Observatory for Justice and Accountability at the University of Guelph, and E. Fuller-Thomson, et al., "The Association between Adverse Childhood Experiences (ACEs) and Suicide Attempts in a Population-based Study," *Child: Care, Health and Development* 42, no. 5 (2016): 725-34.

manifests itself later in chronic illnesses, a higher risk of suicide, and a far greater likelihood of being victims or perpetrators of intimate-partner violence. This creates a huge societal cost, as well as an economic cost.

Another aspect of intimate partner violence that needs to be discussed is that it transcends nationalities, religions, and socioeconomic brackets. That last category often trips people up. It's hard to wrap your head around "upscale violence" or "affluent violence," terms coined by the American psychologist Susan Weitzman in her 2000 book *"Not to People Like Us": Hidden Abuse in Upscale Marriages.*

Research tends to focus on women believed to be the most vulnerable: immigrants, Indigenous women, impoverished women. We believe, wrongly, that it's easy for an affluent woman to leave an abusive situation, that "high-achieving" women have the money and the support systems to walk away. We think she can pack up and check into the best hotel in town. A woman seen to be affluent and successful is far more likely to get the questions all women who disclose an abusive relationship inevitably face: "Why didn't you leave earlier?" or "How could you expose your children to that situation?" (We never ask, "Why did he abuse?")

Yet high-profile stories of women like Nicole Brown Simpson and Reeva Steenkamp suggest otherwise. The cookbook author and TV personality Nigella Lawson divorced her husband Charles Saatchi soon after photographs of them arguing on a restaurant patio were released: his hand was wrapped around her throat. Saatchi later accepted a caution for assault and called it a "playful tiff." I've been there. There's nothing "playful" about it.

We're finally starting to see upscale violence portrayed in popular culture, most notably in *Big Little Lies*, the HBO series. Watching it, I felt sick but I couldn't look away. It was if the producers had filmed my life. I felt the same way hearing about the December 2016 murder of Dr. Elana Fric, a Toronto family physician and mother of three. Her husband, Mohammed Shamji, a neurosurgeon, beat her then choked her to death two days after she served him with divorce papers. Shamji pleaded guilty to second-degree murder in 2019. From the outside, on social media, they looked like a happy couple. A profile of their marriage in *Toronto Life* magazine, written after the murder, featured so many parallels to my own it made me physically ill: the belittling comments, the emotional abuse, the controlling behaviour, the choking and physical assaults.

Until fairly recently, affluent abuse hadn't received much attention or research due to biases held by police, social services, and the general public. Sagesse, a Calgary organization dedicated to helping women recover from domestic violence, has recognized a clear gap in services and supports for affluent women. Andrea Silverstone, the co-chair of the Calgary Domestic Violence Collective, has noted that service providers often fail to see the vulnerability of this population because "they are not accustomed to associating risk or helplessness with privileged populations." The vast majority of mental health care spending goes to the sliver of the population that most obviously need it: the homeless and visibly mentally ill. Those people need help, but they are not the only ones in need.

Affluent women, in fact, may have more difficulties than most in facing up to their problems. Their internalized privilege can lead to denial, and an unwillingness to identify with marginalized women who've gone through comparable trauma. Affluent women often feel a need to protect the abuser's social standing and income. There's the fear the victim won't be believed if the abuser is a pillar of the community, and that the abuser's influence and connections could be used to ruin the victim. And then there's the financial control, legal controls, and technological surveillance that often figure into "affluent" abuse, as it did with me.

Because of the "battered woman" stereotype, it took me more than a decade to even understand that I was in an abusive marriage. Again, I had no bruises. What I had experienced for years before the abuse became physical, and after that, was coercive, controlling behaviour in the form of constant emotional threats and verbal humiliation, what the specialists in domestic violence call "intimate terrorism." It isn't one event—it's a process that erodes your sense of self and your personal agency. It puts you constantly on edge, leaves you afraid even in your own home. Even when I did have bruises, it took years to understand how trauma bonding, an addiction in itself, kept me anchored to an unhealthy situation.

After George's death, I became an advocate for awareness and improved services for mental illness and people who have substance addictions. For more than a year, I've given speeches, participated in seminars, worked with the City of Calgary and the Government of Alberta, and filmed a public service announcement with my daughter Isla.

In my advocacy work, I concentrate on the problems around trying to see mental illness and addiction in their entirety. Mental illness and addiction are chronic conditions and while recovery is possible, it is not without a lot of hard work and support. We need to start meeting both our mental health and illness needs in a coordinated and committed manner that involves all levels of government, health care, justice, corrections and policing, education, employment, public and private and social sectors, schools, communities, and philanthropic agencies. We need a deeper understanding of the lived experience of both the traumatized individual and the family unit in order to plan and deliver good services. Meeting community needs is as important as providing medical needs; something that should be self-evident. If there is a continuum of care in all sectors and at any age and any stage, there would not be such demand for medical care and policing at a point of crisis.

I take this holistic approach because I'm haunted by the "what ifs" of George's life. What if he had been unable to go to the Scripps Clinic in California and instead had had coordinated care in Canada, reporting to one person? What if that naturopath had not given him steroids? What if the Foothills Medical Centre in Calgary had coordinated with all the clinicians working with him? What if George had been introduced sooner to DBT (dialectical behavorial therapy), known to be effective in treating borderline personality disorder? The list goes on.

There has been positive movement. In June 2018, I met the mayor of Calgary, Naheed Nenshi, who has been very supportive. During our first conversation, I said we needed, as a city, to do more for people suffering with mental illness and addiction, noting how difficult the system is to navigate, that everything is there but no one knows how to access it. He told me he wanted to enact a ten-year plan similar to the city's homeless strategy. Two months later, he proposed a notice of motion to allocate $25 million over a five-to-ten-year plan to address mental health and addiction. In 2019, the City of Calgary approved a Community Action on Mental

Health and Addiction (CAMHA) and appointed a community-based stewardship group. I was honored to be named a co-chair with Dr. Chris Eagle.

Also in 2019, as part of the Calgary Police Service recognizing domestic violence an "epidemic" after a series of horrific homicides of women by their partners or former partners, it created an app that helps women connect with various support services. But apps are useless without greater societal and systemic focus on ways to eradicate intimate partner and family violence, and that begins with the recognition that no group is immune. The focus should not be on "why women stay" but how we can make sure families are safe. In this regard, we should look to models in both Australia and New Zealand.

Because of George's illness, my children are also committed to changing the system. John will be co-chairing the family foundation with me. Isla volunteers at the Canadian Mental Health Association, or CMHA. She also appeared with me on a public service announcement for the City of Calgary and spoke with me at an event supporting the Women's for Men's Health Group. Carter's summer employment was with CMHA.

Isla's essay, "An Individual's Actions," captures the turmoil experienced by the child of a parent with substance addictions: "During his sober moments, I wished he'd be drunk. During his drunk and abusive states, I wished he'd be sober. Each time he relapsed, I was always the first to notice. It was a gamble I played in my mind, whether I should tell my mom, or leave him be. He seemed happier when he was drunk, but he would slip into a slope of depression and physical and emotional abuse."

Isla understood that George's addiction wasn't only to substances. "He became addicted to anything that showed society how powerful he was and his motives were influenced by displaying to the world he was 'Daddy Warbucks.' In reality, he was the same as the majority of the population, but he wouldn't accept that."

George's life and his death has left a deep imprint on my children. We share with each other the details of our violent nightmares. Isla has learned to draw lines for herself: she won't hang out with friends who are heavy drinkers and drug users, and will always question her own attitude to and management of alcohol. She finds being around those indulging in extreme substance misuse triggering, reminding her of walking her father to bed after he'd passed out at the dinner table.

Bessel van der Kolk, the Dutch psychiatrist who specializes in trauma, once wrote about the profound effect trauma has: "The mind forgets but the body remembers." He's referring to the reflexive responses experienced long after the initial trauma passes, something that has been true for me. My body still responds to the sound of iPhone texts pinging or even the clatter of keyboards, taking me back to the hostile texting back and forth with George.

My body still responds the way it used to with George when somebody speaks to me in a demeaning or forcible way. My heart races, my mind shuts down, I can't form words, and my lips get dry. Sometimes, if I'm strolling through a nice shop, I think of George and feel extreme sadness, with memories of how much significance shopping had for him. It also has been difficult to undo all of the years I spent passing everything through the filter of "What would George think?" He was always that second voice in my head, commenting on what I was wearing, or what I was saying or thinking.

I now notice families walking down the street, revolving around a key character. I see everyone around him (or her) walking on eggshells, and directing conversation toward that person, trying to win his (or her) approval. I can read the dynamic simply by how that person carries themselves: the voice, the words. I see the young ones and their susceptibility to choosing a life like mine. I want to sit them down and warn them to not take twenty-plus years to make that choice.

For me, achieving true forgiveness has been a reckoning of sorts, one that involves a stark appraisal of the pain I experienced combined with a recognition and gratitude for what I have. I am grateful for my family and my children, for their patience and love and open hearts. We plan to keep moving forward, remembering the best of George while using lessons we have learned to help others. That is the vital part of George's legacy that I, and our family, want to share.

I often think of the line in the minister's eulogy to George about "coaxing the darkness of mental illness into the light of day to heal" and of how a true human community welcomes "the whole person, the broken parts and the whole." It's up to all of us now to carry it through.

ACKNOWLEDGEMENTS

I WROTE THIS BOOK IN hopes that others will learn and benefit from my experience. My three children, now young adults, wanted our family's story told, and I have told it with their assistance and by relying on the journals I kept for more than twenty years. I have chosen not to use people's names unless they were in the public domain or consent was given to do so.

I haven't sugar-coated anything. Some of the details will be difficult to read, particularly for anyone who is currently in or who has survived an abusive relationship. But, again, I believe we need to speak plainly and honestly to confront the realities of mental illness and domestic violence. I know many readers will recognize themselves in my story, or recognize someone they know. If it can help one person, particularly a young person, to see life more clearly and to seek help, it will have been worth telling.

My story would not be possible without Ken Whyte and the late Anne Kingston—thank you for believing I had experiences that would help others, and encouraging me to share.

I want to express my gratitude to George Gosbee for the love, hope, and opportunities he gave me; our dear children, John, Carter, and Isla, for their love and support, and for inspiring me to continue to grow and advocate for change; my mother for showing me love, understanding, and the importance of listening; my father for inspiring my continual search for knowledge and resiliency; Scott for the morning calls and all the baking; Kathleen for mentoring independence; John King, my guiding light—I could not have survived without your knowledge, guidance, love, and support; the Zivot family, Rose and Debbie for their generosity, and Mark,

I would not be where I am today without you—I love and appreciate all you do.

Thanks to my warm handholders: Rosalie Lapuz, Michelle Lazo, Paula Davies, Marc Haaf, Damien Kulynych, Spencer Gunning, Archie and Austin Hall, Tucker McKenzie, Stephanie Raptis, Wendy Mullane, James McIntyre, Nima Dorjee, Winston Canham, and Rylee Fieldstone.

Thanks to my community supports: Marilyn Westerman and the late Gertie Bastido, Afzaal Hussain, Matt and Bart Onysko.

Thanks to my cheerleaders: Jane Vernon, Tracey MacMillan, Mark Fitzgerald, Tom Valentine, Peter McLeod, Michael Tims, Eva Klein, Len Waverman, Bob Thompson, Kelly Streit, Carol Ann Williams, Dominic Caracciolo, Raechelle Paperny, and Kara Honsinger.

Thanks to my mental health and addiction gurus and, more important, good friends: Laureen MacNeil, Chris Eagle, Val Taylor, Yared Belayneh, and Steve Hardy.

Finally, thanks to Your Worship Naheed Nenshi, Calgary Councillors, Nancy Close, Melanie Hulsker, Raynell McDonough and Doug Borch for giving me the opportunity to create hope and strengthen support for people, families, and communities living with mental health and addictions.

Karen Gosbee
Calgary, Alberta
2020